CHINESE CRASH COURSE
速成中文

(第一册)
(Volume 1)

于淼　编著
(By Yu Miao)

北京语言大学出版社
BEIJING LANGUAGE AND CULTURE
UNIVERSITY PRESS

(京)新登字 157 号

图书在版编目(CIP)数据

速成中文/于淼编著.—北京:北京语言大学出版社,
2007.6
ISBN 978-7-5619-1808-1

Ⅰ.速… Ⅱ.于… Ⅲ.汉语-对外汉语教学-教材
Ⅳ.H195.4

中国版本图书馆 CIP 数据核字(2007)第 030869 号

书　　名:	速成中文·1
中文编辑:	周鹂
英文编辑:	武思敏
责任印制:	汪学发
出版发行:	北京语言大学出版社
社　　址:	北京市海淀区学院路 15 号　邮政编码:100083
网　　址:	www.blcup.com
电　　话:	发行部　82303650/3591/3651
	编辑部　82303647
	读者服务部　82303653/3908
印　　刷:	北京新丰印刷厂
经　　销:	全国新华书店
版　　次:	2007 年 8 月第 1 版　2007 年 8 月第 1 次印刷
开　　本:	889 毫米×1194 毫米　1/32　印张:8.125
字　　数:	212 千字　印数:1—5000
书　　号:	ISBN 978-7-5619-1808-1/H·07026

凡有印装质量问题,本社负责调换。电话:82303590

前　言

　　如果你是在中国生活的外国人,你如何才能快速进入汉语目的语的交际圈?如何用最短的学习时间达到中级汉语的水平?如何摆脱课堂学习的呆板?如何学到最有用的交际汉语?这一直是困扰"老外"学中文的头疼问题。现在,这套多媒体教材就是专业的对外汉语教师为"老外"制定的最佳学习方案!

　　也许你在中国的工作太忙而没有学习时间,也许你觉得汉字太难,也许你面对出租车司机的俚语感到头疼,也许你听不懂中国同事的书面汉语,那么,现在这套教材就是你最好的老师,因为我们的目的就是:最快地学好最有用的汉语!

　　教材的编写者要努力使"老外"达到"口说书面语"的能力。

　　对话和短文采取了"功能语句强化导入"的方法,即教材所使用的句子都是有较强扩展和搭配能力的核心语句。前两册三十篇课文以对话为主,对话内容包括了外籍人士在华生活或工作的大部分场景,第二册后半部分还安排了一定数量的商务汉语交际;第三册课文的安排主要是考虑到语段的学习,每篇短文不到400字,用记叙、说明、抒情、描写以及故事等各种文体来展现汉语常用的表述方式。

　　三册生词总量达到了1700个,涵盖了所有现代汉语800至1000的高频词。对于补充生词部分,有的给出了相关例句,有的则在之后的课文中复现出来,而第三册的"相关阅读"主要是用相似的话题背景来复现主课文的生词。

　　语法点和语法项目主要以常用例句来说明,并在"句型"部分着重体现。第三册"句型"部分与前两册有所不同,侧重于语句结构。第一册练习中的"完成句子"部分比较灵活,而第三册的练习以词组或词的扩展搭配为主。在练习上,编者力图以少量的练习来强化学习者的功能语句,并帮助学习者进一步使用中级汉语的常用词语。

  本教材配有多媒体软件,她像是一个时刻陪伴着学习者的汉语家教。学习者可以不受时间和空间的限制,轻松愉快地自助学习,达到短期速成的目的。

  本教材侧重于"速成"和"有用",有别于传统的学院式教学模式,目标是力争使学习者短期内达到中级汉语的水平,并在一定的正式交际场合有"口说书面语"的能力,以得体的语句来应对在中国的生活和工作的需要。

编 者

FORWORD

As a foreigner living in China, how can you attain the level of communication in Chinese quickly? How can you reach the intermediate level in the shortest time? How can you get rid of the inflexibility in learning? How can you learn the most useful communicative Chinese? These are all sticking points that have been troubling "the foreigners learning Chinese". Now *Chinese Crash Course*, a series of multimedia textbook compiled by experienced teachers of Chinese as a foreign language will definitely ease your tension in learning Chinese and make your Chinese learning a pleasant and fun experience!

Maybe you are so busy with your work in China that you do not have much time to study. Maybe you think Chinese characters are so hard to learn. Maybe you get a headache when you hear the taxi drivers' slang. Maybe you can't understand the written Chinese of your Chinese colleagues. If so this set of textbooks is your best teacher, because it aims to help you learn the most useful Chinese at the fastest speed!

The editors of the textbook are trying to make foreigners reach the level of "speaking out the written language".

The dialogues and short passages adopt the method of "functional sentences consolidating learning". All the sentences in the textbooks are the core sentences that are extendible to many situations. The first two volumes are mainly dialogues which concern about foreign people's life and work in China. The latter part of the second volume contains a number of dialogues in business communi cation; the third volume concentrates on the learning of paragraphs. Each passage is less than 400 words, illustrating narrative, expository, lyric, descriptive, and other writing styles.

The three volumes have a total vocabulary of 1,700 words and expressions, which cover 800 to 1,000 high frequency words in modern Chinese. As for the supplementary words, some are provided with example sentences and some reappear in latter texts.

"Related Reading" in the third volume is mainly to review the new words of the texts through passages of similar topics. The grammar points are illustrated with example sentences and are emphasized in "Sentence Patterns". "Sentence Patterns" in the third volume, different from the first two volumes, focuses on the sentence structures.

"Complete the sentences" in the exercises in the first volume is rather flexible while the exercises of third volume are mainly about words and phrases extension and collocation. The compilers try to strengthen the functional sentences by exercises and help the learners use the commonly-used words of the intermediate Chinese.

The textbook is accompanied with a multimedia software. It serves as a Chinese tutor who accompanies the learners all the time. With this book in hand, neither time nor space can limit the learners from studying Chinese in a relaxed and pleasant way.

The textbook emphasizes "speeded-up mastery" and "practicality". Different from the traditional classroom teaching, it aims at making the learners reach the intermediate Chinese level in a short period of time. That is "speaking out the written Chinese" under formal occasions and speaking appropriate Chinese to meet the needs of the life and work in China.

The compiler

Contents

目 录
Contents

汉语语音 ·· 1
Chinese Pronunciation

第 1 课   你好！我是大卫。····················· 14
Lesson One   Hello! I'm David.

第 2 课   这是你的电脑吗? ····················· 28
Lesson Two   Is this your computer?

第 3 课   请问,附近有银行吗? ··············· 41
Lesson Three   Excuse me, is there a bank nearby?

第 4 课   我们的生活很幸福! ················· 51
Lesson Four   We lead a happy life!

第 5 课   现在几点了? ··························· 63
Lesson Five   What time is it?

第 6 课   明天晚上你有时间吗? ············· 76
Lesson Six   Do you have time tomorrow evening?

Chinese Crash Course

第 7 课	你要吃点儿什么？............... 89
Lesson Seven	What would you like to eat?

第 8 课	我现在上网看我的邮箱。............ 103
Lesson Eight	I'm checking my mailbox on the internet.

第 9 课	出租车！................... 116
Lesson Nine	Taxi!

第 10 课	这件上衣我最满意！............ 128
Lesson Ten	This is the coat that I am most satisfied with!

第 11 课	我参加了一个中文辅导班。......... 141
Lesson Eleven	I attend a Chinese tutoring class.

第 12 课	您用航空邮寄还是普通邮寄？....... 155
Lesson Twelve	Do you want to post it by air mail or ordinary mail?

第 13 课	请把这些美元存到信用卡里。........ 167
Lesson Thirteen	Please deposit these US dollars in the credit card.

第 14 课	我喜欢太极拳和成龙的电影。........ 181
Lesson Fourteen	I like shadow boxing and the movies of Jackie Chan.

第 15 课	医生，我肚子特别疼！............. 195
Lesson Fifteen	Doctor, I have a bad stomachache!

Contents

生　词	New Words ·································	209
专有名词	Proper Nouns ······························	236
附　录 1 Appendix 1	语法术语对照表 ·························· Abbreviations of Chinese Grammatical Terms	238
附　录 2 Appendix 2	常用反义词 ································ Common Antonyms	239
附　录 3 Appendix 3	汉字书写 ··································· Chinese Writing System	240

汉语语音
CHINESE PRONUNCIATION

The phonetic unit of Chinese pronunciation is the syllable. A Chinese phonetic syllable consists of three parts: the initial, the final and the tone. For example, in mā, m is the initial, a is the final, - is the tone. The corresponding character of mā is 妈 (mother).

1. Alphabets

Aa	Bb	Cc	Dd	Ee	Ff	Gg	Hh	Ii
Jj	Kk	Ll	Mm	Nn	Oo	Pp	Qq	Rr
Ss	Tt	Uu	Vv	Ww	Xx	Yy	Zz	

2. Initials

There are 21 initials in the Chinese language.

b	p	m	f
d	t	n	l
g	k	h	
j	q	x	
zh	ch	sh	r
z	c	s	

Chinese Crash Course

Initials	Similar English Phonemes	Examples in Chinese		
b	like "b" in "bed"	bà	爸	dad
p	like "p" in "pop"	pà	怕	afraid
m	like "m" in "meat"	mā	妈	mom
f	like "f" in "foot"	fēng	风	wind
d	like "d" in "bed"	dà	大	big
t	like "t" in "tea"	tiān	天	sky
n	like "n" in "need"	nǚ	女	woman
l	like "l" in "leaf"	lái	来	come
g	like "g" in "get"	gāo	高	high
k	like "k" in "kill"	kǎ	卡	card
h	like "h" in "hen"	huì	会	meet
j	like "g" in "genius"(unaspirated)	jī	鸡	chicken
q	harder than "ch" in "cheap"	qù	去	go
x	like "sh" in "shirt" but with the corner of the lips drawn back	xī	西	west
zh	like "j" in "job"	zhù	住	live
ch	like "ch" in "match"	chá	茶	tea
sh	like "sh" in "English"	shǒu	手	hand
r	close to "r" in "rain"	rén	人	person
z	like "ds" in "words"	zì	字	character
c	like "ts" in "rats" with aspiration	cū	粗	thick
s	like "s" in "Sunday"	sān	三	three

Chinese Pronunciation

3. Finals

There are 36 finals in the Chinese language.

	i	u	ü
a	ia	ua	
o		uo	
e	ie		üe
er			
ai		uai	
ei		ui(uei)	
ao	iao		
ou	iu(iou)		
an	ian	uan	üan
en	in	un(uen)	ün
ang	iang	uang	
eng	ing	ueng	
ong	iong		

There are 7 simple vowel finals.

Finals	Similar English Phonemes	Examples in Chinese		
a	like "a" in "father"	tā	他	he
o	like "o" in "or"	wǒ	我	I
e	like "ir" in "dirty"	hé	和	and
i	like "i" in "in"	nǐ	你	you
u	like "u" in "blue"	shù	树	tree
ü	no equivalent in English, like "u" in "lune" (French pronunciation)	yú	鱼	fish
er	no equivalent in English	ěr	耳	ear

Chinese Crash Course

There are 13 compound vowel finals.

Finals	Similar English Phonemes	Examples in Chinese		
ai	like "y" in "by"	hǎi	海	sea
ao	like "ow" in "cow"	hǎo	好	good
ei	like "ei" in "eight"	hēi	黑	black
ia	like "yar" in "yard"	jiā	家	home
		yā	鸭	duck
ie	like "ye" in "yes"	xiè	谢	thank
		yě	也	also
iou	like "you"	qiū	秋	autumn
		yǒu	有	have
iao	like "i" in "in" plus "ow" in "cow"	xiǎo	小	small
		yǎo	咬	bite
ou	like "oa" in "coat"	kǒu	口	mouth
ua	like "wa" in "waft"	huā	花	flower
		wā	蛙	frog
uei	like "way"	tuī	推	push
		wèi	喂	feed
uo	like "war"	huǒ	火	fire
		wǒ	我	I
uai	like "why"	huài	坏	bad
		wài	外	outside
üe	no equivalent in English, like "u" in "lune"(French pronunciation) plus "e" in "pet"	xuě	雪	snow
		yuè	月	moon

Chinese Pronunciation

There are 16 nasal finals.

Finals	Similar English Phonemes	Examples in Chinese		
an	like "an" in "land"	shān	山	hill
ang	no equivalent in English, like "an" in "ancien" (French pronunciation)	cháng	长	long
en	like "en" in "stolen"	shēn	深	deep
eng	like "en" in "stolen" plus "ng" in "long"	lěng	冷	cold
ong	like "or" in "worn" plus "ng" in "long"	hóng	红	red
in	like "in"	xīn	新	new
		yīn	因	because
ing	like "ing" in "spring"	jìng	静	quiet
		yīng	鹰	eagle
ian	like "yen"	biàn	变	change
		yǎn	眼	eye
iang	like "young"	xiàng	像	like
		yáng	羊	sheep
iong	like "i" in "bin" plus "ong" in "long"	xióng	熊	bear
		yòng	用	use
uan	like "wan" in "swan"	guān	关	close
		wán	玩	play
uang	no equivalent in English, like "u" in "flute" plus "an" in "ancien" (French pronunciation)	guāng	光	light
		wàng	忘	forget
uen	like "u" in "flute" plus "en" in "stolen"	cún	存	deposit
		wěn	吻	kiss
ueng	like "u" in "flute" plus "ng" in "long"	wēng	嗡	buzz
üan	no equivalent in English, like "u" in "lune" (French pronunciation) plus "an" in "land"	xuǎn	选	choose
		yuǎn	远	far
ün	no equivalent in English, like "u" in "lune" (French pronunciation) plus "n" in "stolen"	qún	裙	skirt
		yún	云	cloud

SUCHENGZHONGWEN 速成中文

Chinese Crash Course

4．普通话声母韵母拼合总表
4. Table of Combinations of Initials and Finals in *Putonghua*

F\I	a	o	e	-i [ɿ]	-i [ʅ]	er	ai	ei	ao	ou	an	en	ang	eng	ong	i	ia	iao	ie
	a	o	e			er	ai	ei	ao	ou	an	en	ang	eng		yi	ya	yao	ye
b	ba	bo					bai	bei	bao		ban	ben	bang	beng		bi		biao	bie
p	pa	po					pai	pei	pao	pou	pan	pen	pang	peng		pi		piao	pie
m	ma	mo	me				mai	mei	mao	mou	man	men	mang	meng		mi		miao	mie
f	fa	fo						fei		fou	fan	fen	fang	feng					
d	da		de				dai	dei	dao	dou	dan	den	dang	deng	dong	di		diao	die
t	ta		te				tai		tao	tou	tan		tang	teng	tong	ti		tiao	tie
n	na		ne				nai	nei	nao	nou	nan	nen	nang	neng	nong	ni		niao	nie
l	la		le				lai	lei	lao	lou	lan		lang	leng	long	li	lia	liao	lie
z	za		ze	zi			zai	zei	zao	zou	zan	zen	zang	zeng	zong				
c	ca		ce	ci			cai		cao	cou	can	cen	cang	ceng	cong				
s	sa		se	si			sai		sao	sou	san	sen	sang	seng	song				
zh	zha		zhe		zhi		zhai	zhei	zhao	zhou	zhan	zhen	zhang	zheng	zhong				
ch	cha		che		chi		chai		chao	chou	chan	chen	chang	cheng	chong				
sh	sha		she		shi		shai	shei	shao	shou	shan	shen	shang	sheng					
r			re		ri				rao	rou	ran	ren	rang	reng	rong				
j																ji	jia	jiao	jie
q																qi	qia	qiao	qie
x																xi	xia	xiao	xie
g	ga		ge				gai	gei	gao	gou	gan	gen	gang	geng	gong				
k	ka		ke				kai	kei	kao	kou	kan	ken	kang	keng	kong				
h	ha		he				hai	hei	hao	hou	han	hen	hang	heng	hong				

Chinese Pronunciation

iu	ian	in	iang	ing	iong	u	ua	uo	uai	ui	uan	un	uang	ueng	ü	üe	üan	ün
you	yan	yin	yang	ying	yong	wu	wa	wo	wai	wei	wan	wen	wang	weng	yu	yue	yuan	yun
	bian	bin		bing		bu												
	pian	pin		ping		pu												
miu	mian	min		ming		mu												
						fu												
diu	dian			ding		du		duo		dui	duan	dun						
	tian			ting		tu		tuo		tui	tuan	tun						
niu	nian	nin	niang	ning		nu		nuo			nuan				nü	nüe		
liu	lian	lin	liang	ling		lu		luo			luan	lun			lü	lüe		
						zu		zuo		zui	zuan	zun						
						cu		cuo		cui	cuan	cun						
						su		suo		sui	suan	sun						
						zhu	zhua	zhuo	zhuai	zhui	zhuan	zhun	zhuang					
						chu	chua	chuo	chuai	chui	chuan	chun	chuang					
						shu	shua	shuo	shuai	shui	shuan	shun	shuang					
						ru	rua	ruo		rui	ruan	run						
jiu	jian	jin	jiang	jing	jiong										ju	jue	juan	jun
qiu	qian	qin	qiang	qing	qiong										qu	que	quan	qun
xiu	xian	xin	xiang	xing	xiong										xu	xue	xuan	xun
						gu	gua	guo	guai	gui	guan	gun	guang					
						ku	kua	kuo	kuai	kui	kuan	kun	kuang					
						hu	hua	huo	huai	hui	huan	hun	huang					

Chinese Crash Course

5. Tones

In Chinese the variation of a syllable's tone may distinguish meaning. For example, mǎi 买 (to buy) and mài 卖 (to sell). There are four tones in Chinese, and they are repersented by ‾ ´ ˇ ` .

tone category	tone mark	characteristics of the tones	examples
high level	‾	starting high and keeping level	mā 妈 (mother)
rising	´	rising from middle to high	má 麻 (hemp)
falling and rising	ˇ	first falling then rising	mǎ 马 (horse)
falling	`	starting high and falling abruptly	mà 骂 (scold)

6. Rules for Chinese *Pinyin*

(1) The final i after z, c, s or zh, ch, sh, r is not pronounced as [i], instead, it should be pronounced as -i[ɿ] or -i[ʅ].

For example, sì 四, shì 是, rì 日. They sound like the prolonged friction of the initials, which change from voiceless sounds into voiced sounds. Please pay attention to the pronunciation of i in following cases.

Practice pronouncing the following syllables:

Chinese Pronunciation

bī	pī	mī	dī	tī	nī
lī	jī	qī	xī	zhī	chī
shī	rī	zī	cī	sī	

(2) ① When a final started with ü is preceded by j, q, x, the two dots above are dropped. That means the u after j, q, x should be pronounced as ü rather than u.

jù	qǔ	xū
句	曲	须
sentence	tune	must

② The two dots above ü should be kept if it follows n and l.

nǚ	Lǚ
女	吕
female	a surname

③ When there is no initial before the final ü, we add the quasi-initial y before it and meanwhile remove the dots.

üan→	yuān	yuán	yuǎn	yuàn
	渊	园	远	愿
	deep	garden	far	wish

ü→	yu	yú	yǔ	yù
	淤	鱼	雨	遇
	stasis	fish	rain	meet

Chinese Crash Course

(3) The finals in the forms of iu, ui and un are actually short forms for iou, uei, uen. Please pay attention to their pronunciations.

niú	shuǐ	hūn
牛	水	昏
cow	water	faint

(4) When a tone mark needs to be added above i, the dot above should be removed.

yìqǐ	dǐxì	bǐlì	sīlì
一起	底细	比例	私立
together	ins and outs	proportion	private-run

(5) When a syllable beginning with a, o, e follows another syllable, the dividing mark (') should be used.

Xī'ān
西安
Xi'an City

(6) When there is no initial before a compound final started with i in a syllable, we change i into the quasi-initial y.

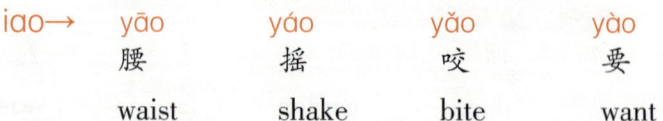

iao→	yāo	yáo	yǎo	yào
	腰	摇	咬	要
	waist	shake	bite	want

If there is no other vowel, we need to add y before i.

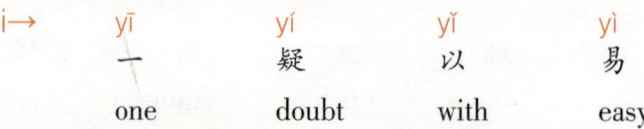

i→	yī	yí	yǐ	yì
	一	疑	以	易
	one	doubt	with	easy

Chinese Pronunciation

(7) When there is no initial before a compound final started with u, u needs to be changed into w.

uan→	wān	wán	wǎn	wàn
	弯	完	晚	万
	bend	finish	late	ten thousand

And if there is no other vowel behind u, w should be added before u.

u→	wū	wú	wǔ	wù
	屋	无	五	物
	house	without	five	object

(8) The syllables standing for one word should be grouped together in spelling.

shìjiè   dìtú
世界   地图
world   map

A space is needed between two words.

xǐ yīfu   kàn diànshì
洗 衣服   看 电视
wash clothes   watch TV

Capitalize the initial letter of a proper noun. If the proper noun is made up of several words, all the initial letters of these words should be capitalized.

Zhōngguó   Fǎlánkèfú   Běijīng Fàndiàn
中国   法兰克福   北京饭店
China   Frankfurt   Beijing Hotel

Chinese Crash Course

In spelling Chinese people's names, there should be a space between the surname and the given name. Capitalize the initial letters of both parts.

Dèng Xiǎopíng
邓　小平
Deng Xiaoping

Fùlánkèlín Luósīfú
富兰克林·罗斯福
Franklin Roosevelt

7. Pronunciation Exercises

bàba 爸爸 daddy	měimǎn 美满 satisfactory	fāngfǎ 方法 method	piānpáng 偏旁 radical
dàodé 道德 moral	tuántǐ 团体 group	niúnǎi 牛奶 milk	liúlì 流利 fluent
gǎigé 改革 reform	kāngkǎi 慷慨 generous	jiějué 解决 solve	qiàqiǎo 恰巧 accidentally
xíngxiàng 形象 image	zhēnzhèng 真正 true	zuìzé 罪责 crime	huánghūn 黄昏 dusk
róngrěn 容忍 tolerate	cāngcù 仓促 haste	hǎi'ōu 海鸥 seagull	chuōchuān 戳穿 expose

Chinese Pronunciation

sōusuǒ	ānwěn	fáng'ài	ángyáng
搜索	安稳	妨碍	昂扬
search	stable	hinder	high spirited

shānshuǐ
山水
mountains and waters

Dì Yī Kè Nǐ hǎo! Wǒ shì Dàwèi.
第 1 课 你好！我是大卫。
Lesson One Hello! I'm David.

 **Sentence Patterns**

1. Nǐ hǎo!
   你 好！

   Hello!

2. Lǎoshī, nín hǎo!
   老 师，您 好！

   Hello, teacher!

3. Nín guìxìng?
   您 贵 姓？

   What's your family name please?

4. Nǐ jiào shénme míngzi?
   你 叫 什 么 名 字？

   What's your name?

5. Wǒ xìng Wáng, wǒ jiào Wáng Yǔ.
   我 姓 王，我 叫 王 宇。

   My family name is Wang. My name is Wang Yu.

   (Wǒ de míngzi shì Wáng Yǔ.)
   (我 的 名 字 是 王 宇。)

   (My name is Wang Yu.)

Lesson One Hello! I'm David.

6. Qǐngwèn nǐ shì nǎ guó rén?
   请 问 你 是 哪 国 人?

   Excuse me, where do you come from?

7. Wǒ shì Měiguórén.
   我 是 美 国 人。

   I come from America.

8. Nǐ ne?
   你 呢?

   How about you?

9. Tāmen yě shì Yīngguórén ma?
   他 们 也 是 英 国 人 吗?

   Are they also from the United Kingdom?

10. Tā shì shuí? Wǒ bú rènshi tā.
    他 是 谁? 我 不 认 识 他。

    Who's he? I don't know him.

11. Rènshi nǐ hěn gāoxìng.
    认 识 你 很 高 兴。

    Nice to meet you.

12. Huānyíng nǐ lái Zhōngguó.
    欢 迎 你 来 中 国。

    Welcome to China.

13. Xièxie.
    谢 谢。

    Thanks.

Chinese Crash Course

 **Dialogues**

A: Lǎoshī, nín hǎo!
老师，您好！
Hello, teacher!

B: Nǐ hǎo! Qǐngwèn nǐ jiào shénme míngzi?
你好！请问你叫什么名字？
Hello! What's your name, please?

A: Wǒ jiào Dàwèi. Qǐngwèn nín guìxìng?
我叫大卫。请问您贵姓？
My name is David. What's your family name, please?

Lesson One Hello! I'm David.

B：Wǒ xìng Wáng. Rènshi nǐ hěn gāoxìng.
我 姓 王。认 识 你 很 高 兴。

My family name is Wang. Nice to meet you.

A：Wǒ yě hěn gāoxìng rènshi nín.
我 也 很 高 兴 认 识 您。

Nice to meet you too.

B：Huānyíng nǐ lái Zhōngguó.
欢 迎 你 来 中 国。

Welcome to China.

A：Xièxie!
谢 谢！

Thanks!

A：Nǐ hǎo, qǐngwèn nǐ shì nǎ guó rén?
你 好，请 问 你 是 哪 国 人？

Hello, would you please tell me where you are from?

B：Wǒ shì Àodàlìyàrén, nǐ ne?
我 是 澳 大 利 亚 人，你 呢？

I'm from Australia. And you?

A：Wǒ shì Měiguórén. Wǒ jiào Dàwèi.
我 是 美 国 人。我 叫 大 卫。

I'm American. I'm David.

B：Tā yě shì Měiguórén ma?
她 也 是 美 国 人 吗？

Is she also an American?

Chinese Crash Course

A: Bú shì, tā shì Yīngguórén.
不是，她是英国人。

No, she's British.

B: Qǐngwèn, tā shì shuí?
请问，他是谁？

Excuse me, may I ask who he is?

A: Tā shì wǒmen de Hànyǔ lǎoshī, jiào Wáng Yǔ.
他是我们的汉语老师，叫王宇。

He's our Chinese teacher. His name is Wang Yu.

 **New Words**

1. 老师　　lǎoshī　　名 (n.)　　　teacher
2. 您　　　nín　　　　代 (pron.)　　you (respectful form of "你")

Lesson One Hello! I'm David.

3. 你好	nǐ hǎo		hello
你	nǐ	代 (pron.)	you
好	hǎo	形 (adj.)	good
4. 请问	qǐngwèn	动 (v.)	excuse me
问	wèn	动 (v.)	ask
5. 叫	jiào	动 (v.)	be named
6. 什么	shénme	代 (pron.)	what
7. 名字	míngzi	名 (n.)	name
8. 我	wǒ	代 (pron.)	I
9. 贵姓	guìxìng	名 (n.)	your surname
10. 姓	xìng	名、动 (n./v.)	surname; surname
11. 王	Wáng	名 (n.)	a surname
12. 认识	rènshi	动 (v.)	know
13. 很	hěn	副 (adv.)	very
14. 高兴	gāoxìng	动 (v.)	glad, be happy
15. 也	yě	副 (adv.)	also, too
16. 欢迎	huānyíng	动 (v.)	welcome
17. 来	lái	动 (v.)	come
18. 谢谢	xièxie	动 (v.)	thank
19. 是	shì	动 (v.)	be
20. 哪	nǎ	代 (pron.)	which
21. 国	guó	名 (n.)	country
22. 人	rén	名 (n.)	person

Chinese Crash Course

23.	呢	ne	助 (part.)	*modal particle*
24.	她	tā	代 (pron.)	she, her
25.	吗	ma	助 (part.)	*modal particle*
26.	不	bù	副 (adv.)	no
27.	他	tā	代 (pron.)	he, him
28.	谁	shuí/shéi	代 (pron.)	who
29.	我们	wǒmen	代 (pron.)	we, us
	们	men	尾(suf.)	*suffix*
30.	汉语	Hànyǔ	名 (n.)	Chinese

Proper Nouns

1.	大卫	Dàwèi	David
2.	中国	Zhōngguó	China
3.	澳大利亚	Àodàlìyà	Australia
4.	美国	Měiguó	America
5.	英国	Yīngguó	Great Britain
6.	王宇	Wáng Yǔ	Wang Yu

Lesson One Hello! I'm David.

Annotations

1. 您   nín

"Nín" is an honorific title for "nǐ". Generally it's used for eldership or valued people. It is also a polite usage. For example:

您是李老师？
Are you Teacher Li?
您贵姓？
What's your surname?

2. 请问   qǐngwèn

It is used when people want to arouse other person's attention and ask some questions. It's a polite usage. For example:

请问,您是哪国人？
Excuse me, where do you come from?
请问贵姓？
Excuse me, what's your surname?
请问,他的名字是什么？
Excuse me, what's his name?

3. 什么   shénme

It can be put after a verb or before a noun or pronoun to ask questions. For example:

Chinese Crash Course

他姓什么?
What's his surname?
她叫什么名字?
What's her name?

4. 贵姓  guìxìng

It's a polite usage for asking a person's surname. "Guì" indicates noble and respect.

5. 呢 ne

"Ne" is put after a pronoun or a person's name to express the same question just asked. For example:

A：他是美国人,你呢?
    He is an American. And you?
B：我是澳大利亚人。
    I'm an Australian.
A：您贵姓?
    What's your surname?
B：我姓王。
    My surname is Wang.
A：你呢?
    And you?
C：我姓铃木。
    My surname is Suzuki.

If there is no question asked before, "ne" means where. For example:

Lesson One Hello! I'm David.

A：李老师呢？

　　Where's Teacher Li?

B：他不在。

　　He isn't here.

6. 吗　　ma

"Ma" indicates interrogation. It is usually put at the end of a question. For example:

她是汉语老师吗？

Is she a Chinese teacher?

你们是澳大利亚人吗？

Are you Australians?

他是中国学生吗？

Is he a Chinese student?

7. 不　　bù

"Bù" is used for negation. It can be used independently, and can also be used before verbs or adjectives. For example:

A：您是汉语老师吗？

　　Are you a Chinese teacher?

B：不是。

　　No.

我不姓金，我姓李。

My surname is Li, not Jin.

他们不是日本人。

They aren't Japanese.

Chinese Crash Course

8. 谁　shuí/shéi

It is an interrogative pronoun. For example:

A：他们是谁？
Who are they?

B：他们是美国学生。
They are American students.

A：谁是汉语老师？
Who's the Chinese teacher?

B：李丽。
Li Li.

A：请问谁姓金？
Excuse me, whose surname is Jin?

B：我。
Me.

9. 们　men

"Men" is used after a pronoun or noun that indicates plurality. For example:

我——我们	I——we
你——你们	you——you
老师——老师们	teacher——teachers
学生——学生们	student——students

Lesson One Hello! I'm David.

一 完成句子 Complete the following sentences.

1. A：你好,请问(　　　　)?
   B：我姓(　　　　),我叫(　　　　)。

2. A：你好,请问(　　　　)?
   B：我(　　　　)美国人。

3. A：我是中国人,你呢?
   B：我是(　　　　)。

4. 老师：你(　　　　)好! 我是汉语老师。

5. 他是(　　　　)? 我不认识他。

二 选择 Choose the correct answers.

1. (　　)是王宇老师?
   A 什么　　　B 吗　　　C 谁　　　D 呢

2. 他是大卫(　　)?
   A 呢　　　B 谁　　　C 什么　　　D 吗

3. A：您好,请问您贵姓?
   B：(　　　　)。
   A 谢谢。　　B 我姓李。　　C 你好!　　D 我姓贵。

4. 你(　　)他吗?
   A 也是　　　B 不　　　C 认识　　　D 谁

Chinese Crash Course

5. A：你好，我是英国人，你呢？
   B：(　　　)。
   A 我是老师。　B 我是美国人。　C 我美国人。　D 我呢。

6. 请问你们是(　　　)?
   A 哪学生　　　B 哪国　　　　C 哪国人　　　D 呢

Supplementary Words

1.	介绍	jièshào	动 (v.)	introduce
2.	来自	lái zì		come from
3.	先	xiān	副 (adv.)	first
4.	请	qǐng	动 (v.)	please
5.	多	duō	形 (adj.)	many
6.	关照	guānzhào	动 (v.)	look after
7.	学生	xuésheng	名 (n.)	student
8.	艾玛	Àimǎ	专名 (pn)	Emma
9.	互相	hùxiāng	副 (adv.)	each other
10.	瑞典	Ruìdiǎn	专名 (pn)	Sweden
11.	韩国	Hánguó	专名 (pn)	South Korea
12.	法国	Fǎguó	专名 (pn)	France
13.	俄罗斯	Éluósī	专名 (pn)	Russia
14.	日本	Rìběn	专名 (pn)	Japan

Lesson One   Hello!   I'm David.

Related Sentences

1. 我来介绍一下,这位是王先生。
   Wǒ lái jièshào yíxià, zhè wèi shì Wáng xiānsheng.
   Let me introduce. This is Mr. Wang.

2. 我来自日本。
   Wǒ lái zì Rìběn.
   I come from Japan.

3. 我先自我介绍一下。
   Wǒ xiān zìwǒ jièshào yíxià.
   Let me introduce myself first.

4. 很荣幸认识您,请您多关照。
   Hěn róngxìng rènshi nín, qǐng nín duō guānzhào.
   I am honoured to meet you.

5. 我是澳大利亚学生艾玛。
   Wǒ shì Àodàlìyà xuésheng Àimǎ.
   I'm Emma, a student from Australia.

6. 我们互相认识一下吧。
   Wǒmen hùxiāng rènshi yíxià ba.
   Let's get to know each other.

Dì Èr Kè Zhè shì nǐ de diànnǎo ma?
第 2 课 这是你的电脑吗?
Lesson Two   Is this your computer?

Zhè shì shénme?
1. 这 是 什 么?

   What's this?

Zhèxiē shì Hànyǔ kèběn.
2. 这 些 是 汉 语 课 本。

   These are Chinese textbooks.

Zhè shì nǐ de bǐjìběn diànnǎo ma?
3. 这 是 你 的 笔 记 本 电 脑 吗?

   Is this your laptop computer?

Zhèxiē dōu shì wǒ de.
4. 这 些 都 是 我 的。

   These are all mine.

Nà shì shénme dìfang?
5. 那 是 什 么 地 方?

   What is that place?

Nàli shì yínháng.
6. 那 里 是 银 行。

   That is a bank.

Lesson Two Is this your computer?

Wǒ xiǎng qù chī fàn.
7. 我 想 去 吃 饭。

I want to have a meal.

Zàijiàn!
8. 再 见!

See you later!

Wǎngbā zài chāoshì de qiánmian.
9. 网 吧 在 超 市 的 前 面。

The internet cafe is in front of the supermarket.

Bú kèqi!
10. 不 客 气!

You're welcome!

Dialogues

Àimǎ, zhè shì shénme?
A: 艾 玛, 这 是 什 么?

Emma, what's this?

Zhè shì wǒ de Hànyǔ kèběn.
B: 这 是 我 的 汉 语 课 本。

This is my Chinese textbook.

Chinese Crash Course

A： Zhè shì nǐ de bǐjìběn diànnǎo ma?
这 是 你 的 笔 记 本 电 脑 吗？

Is this your laptop computer?

B： Duì, shì wǒ de.
对，是 我 的。

Yes, it's mine.

A： Nà shì shénme cídiǎn?
那 是 什 么 词 典？

What kind of dictionary is that?

B： Nà shì Yīngyǔ cídiǎn.
那 是 英 语 词 典。

That's an English dictionary.

A： Zhèxiē CD shì shuí de?
这 些 CD 是 谁 的？

Whose CDs are these?

Lesson Two Is this your computer?

B: Dōu shì wǒ de.
都 是 我 的。

They're all mine.

A: Lǐ Lì, nà shì shénme dìfang?
李 丽，那 是 什 么 地 方？

Li Li, what is that place?

B: Nàli shì yínháng.
那 里 是 银 行。

That is a bank.

A: Zhèbiān shì fàndiàn ma?
这 边 是 饭 店 吗？

Is it a restaurant here?

B: Bú shì, zhè shì wǎngbā.
   不是，这是网吧。

No, this is an internet cafe.

A: Fàndiàn zài nǎr?
   饭店在哪儿？

Where is the restaurant?

B: Zài xuéxiào ménkǒu.
   在学校门口。

It is by the gate of the school.

A: Wǒ xiǎng qù chī fàn. Nǐ qù ma?
   我想去吃饭。你去吗？

I want to have a meal. Do you want to go?

B: Wǒ bú qù, zàijiàn!
   我不去，再见！

No, I don't. See you later!

A: Zàijiàn!
   再见！

See you!

A: Qǐngwèn, túshūguǎn zài nǎr?
   请问，图书馆在哪儿？

Excuse me, where is the library?

Lesson Two Is this your computer?

B: Zài nàbiān.
在 那 边。

It's over there.

A: Chāoshì yě zài nàbiān ma?
超 市 也 在 那 边 吗?

Is the supermarket over there too?

B: Duì, chāoshì zài túshūguǎn de qiánbian.
对, 超 市 在 图 书 馆 的 前 边。

Yes. The supermarket is in front of the library.

A: Xièxie!
谢 谢!

Thank you!

B: Bú kèqi!
不 客 气!

You are welcome!

Chinese Crash Course

 **New Words**

1. 这	zhè	代 (pron.)	this
2. 的	de	助 (part.)	*particle*
3. 课本	kèběn	名 (n.)	textbook
4. 笔记本电脑	bǐjìběn diànnǎo		laptop computer
笔记本	bǐjìběn	名 (n.)	notebook
电脑	diànnǎo	名 (n.)	computer
5. 对	duì	形 (adj.)	right
6. 那	nà	代 (pron.)	that
7. 词典/辞典	cídiǎn/cídiǎn	名 (n.)	dictionary
8. 英语	Yīngyǔ	名 (n.)	English
9. 些	xiē	量 (mw)	some
10. 都	dōu	副 (adv.)	all
11. 地方	dìfang	名 (n.)	place
12. 里	lǐ	名 (n.)	inside
13. 银行	yínháng	名 (n.)	bank
14. 边	biān	名 (n.)	side
15. 饭店	fàndiàn	名 (n.)	restaurant
16. 网吧	wǎngbā	名 (n.)	internet cafe
17. 哪儿	nǎr	代 (pron.)	where
18. 学校	xuéxiào	名 (n.)	school

Lesson Two Is this your computer?

19. 门口	ménkǒu	名 (n.)	gate
20. 想	xiǎng	动 (v.)	want
21. 去	qù	动 (v.)	go
22. 吃饭	chī fàn		have a meal
23. 再见	zàijiàn	动 (v.)	good-bye
24. 图书馆	túshūguǎn	名 (n.)	library
25. 超市	chāoshì	名 (n.)	supermarket
26. 前边	qiánbian	名 (n.)	in front of
27. 不客气	bú kèqi		You are welcome.

Annotations

1. 的   de

The structural particle "de" must be used between the attributive and the noun being modified. For example:

这是我的电脑。

This is my computer.

那是谁的课本？

Whose textbook is that?

这是学校的网吧。

This is the internet cafe of the school.

It can be used to represent the person or thing mentioned earlier.

Chinese Crash Course

这是他的东西,我的(东西)在那边。

This is his stuff. Mine is over there.

电脑在这儿。这是他的,那是我的。

The computers are here. This is his and that is mine.

2. 些   xiē

"Xiē" indicates an indefinite amount. For example:

这些课本是我的。

These textbooks are mine.

我不认识那些人。

I don't know those people.

3. "不"的变调   "bù" de biàndiào

The negative adverb "bù" is pronounced as the fourth tone. But when it is followed by a fourth tone character, it is pronounced as the second tone. For example:

不是 bú shì not   不对 bú duì incorrect

4. 在   zài

"Zài" is used as a verb here. It indicates location and orientation. For example:

李老师在这儿。

Teacher Li is here.

我的词典不在那儿。

My dictionary isn't there.

Lesson Two Is this your computer?

网吧在饭店的前边。

The internet cafe is in front of the restaurant.

我的电脑在哪儿?

Where is my computer?

5. When "lǐ", "biān" or "ér" is put after the demonstrative pronouns, "zhè", "nà" and the interrogative pronoun "nǎ", they indicate place or direction.

这里	这边	这儿	here
那里	那边	那儿	there
哪里	哪边	哪儿	where

6. 不客气   *bú kèqi*

It is an answer to "xièxie".

 Chinese Crash Course

 **Exercises**

一 完成句子 Complete the following sentences.

1. A：这是谁的词典？
   B：(　　　　　)。
2. A：那是图书馆吗？
   B：不是,(　　　　　)。
3. A：网吧在哪儿？
   B：(　　　　　)。

二 选择 Choose the correct answers.

1. (　　)是你的笔记本吗？
   A 这　　　B 他　　　C 谁　　　D 我
2. 饭店(　　)超市前面。
   A 在　　　B 是　　　C 不是　　D 的
3. 我的词典在(　　)？
   A 那　　　B 哪儿　　C 什么　　D 谁

三 选词填空 Fill in the following blanks with the proper words.

　　吃饭　　想　　去　　哪儿

1. 我们(　　)图书馆吧。
2. 我想去(　　)。
3. 我不(　　)去网吧。
4. 你想去(　　)？

Lesson Two   Is this your computer?

Supplementary Words

1.	书店	shūdiàn	名 (n.)	bookstore
2.	商店	shāngdiàn	名 (n.)	store
3.	邮局	yóujú	名 (n.)	post office
4.	宿舍	sùshè	名 (n.)	dormitory
5.	房间	fángjiān	名 (n.)	room
6.	后面	hòumian	名 (n.)	back
7.	上网	shàng//wǎng	动 (v.)	get on the internet

Related Sentences

1. 这是我的房间，那是他的。
   Zhè shì wǒ de fángjiān, nà shì tā de.
   This is my room and that is his.
2. 这是什么课本？
   Zhè shì shénme kèběn?
   What textbook is this?
3. 那些不是CD，都是DVD。
   Nàxiē bú shì CD, dōu shì DVD.
   Those aren't CDs, they're DVDs.

Chinese Crash Course

4. 我不想去网吧上网。
   Wǒ bù xiǎng qù wǎngbā shàngwǎng.
   I don't want to get on the internet in an internet cafe.

5. 商店在什么地方？
   Shāngdiàn zài shénme dìfang?
   Where is the store?

6. 你现在去哪儿？
   Nǐ xiànzài qù nǎr?
   Where are you going now?

7. A：多谢！
   Duō xiè!
   Thanks a lot!

   B：不用谢。
   Búyòng xiè.
   You're welcome.

第 3 课 请问，附近有银行吗？
Dì Sā Kè Qǐngwèn, fùjìn yǒu yínháng ma?

Lesson Three Excuse me, is there a bank nearby?

Sentence Patterns

1. 这个包里有什么东西？
   Zhège bāo li yǒu shénme dōngxi?

   What are the things in this bag?

2. 桌子上有一支笔。
   Zhuōzi shang yǒu yì zhī bǐ.

   There is a pen on the desk.

3. 我现在没有钱了。
   Wǒ xiànzài méiyǒu qián le.

   I don't have money now.

4. 请问这儿附近有银行吗？
   Qǐngwèn zhèr fùjìn yǒu yínháng ma?

   Excuse me, is there a bank near here?

5. 在前面的路口往右拐。
   Zài qiánmian de lùkǒu wǎng yòu guǎi.

   Go ahead and turn right at the crossroad.

6. 那个银行旁边就有超市。
   Nàge yínháng pángbiān jiù yǒu chāoshì.

   There is a supermarket next to the bank.

Chinese Crash Course

Dialogues

A: Zhège bāo li yǒu shénme dōngxi?
这个包里有什么东西？

What are the things in this bag?

B: Yǒu yí ge zhàoxiàngjī hé jǐ běn shū.
有一个照相机和几本书。

There is a camera and some books.

A: Zhuōzi shang yǒu yì zhī bǐ, shì shuí de?
桌子上有一支笔，是谁的？

Lesson Three Excuse me, is there a bank nearby?

There is a pen on the desk. Whose pen is this?

B: Bù zhīdào, bú shì wǒ de.
    不 知 道, 不 是 我 的。

I don't know. It's not mine.

A: Wǒ xiànzài méiyǒu qián le, wǒ qù yínháng.
    我 现 在 没 有 钱 了, 我 去 银 行。

I don't have any money now. I'm going to the bank.

B: Nǐ zhīdào zài nǎr ma?
    你 知 道 在 哪 儿 吗?

Do you know where it is?

Chinese Crash Course

Wǒ kěyǐ wèn biéren.
A：我 可 以 问 别 人。

I may ask other people.

Qǐngwèn, zhèr fùjìn yǒu yínháng ma?
A：请 问，这 儿 附 近 有 银 行 吗？

Excuse me, is there a bank near here?

Yǒu, zài qiánmian de lùkǒu wǎng yòu guǎi.
B：有，在 前 面 的 路 口 往 右 拐。

Yes. Go ahead and turn right at the crossroad.

Zài dì yī ge lùkǒu ma?
A：在 第 一 个 路 口 吗？

At the first crossroad?

Lesson Three Excuse me, is there a bank nearby?

B：Duì, nàge hónglǜdēng jiù shì.
   对，那 个 红 绿 灯 就 是。

Yes. Just at that traffic lights.

A：Zài wèn yíxià, fùjìn yǒu chāoshì ma?
   再 问 一 下，附 近 有 超 市 吗?

By the way, is there a supermarket near here?

B：Nàge yínháng pángbiān jiù yǒu chāoshì.
   那 个 银 行 旁 边 就 有 超 市。

There is a supermarket next to the bank.

A：Duō xiè!
   多 谢!

Thanks a lot!

B：Bú kèqi!
   不 客 气!

You're welcome!

New Words

1. 包	bāo	名 (n.)	bag
2. 有	yǒu	动 (v.)	have
3. 东西	dōngxi	名 (n.)	thing
4. 个	gè	量 (mw)	*measure word*
5. 照相机	zhàoxiàngjī	名 (n.)	camera
6. 和	hé	连、介 (conj./prep.)	and

Chinese Crash Course

7.	几	jǐ	代 (pron.)	several
8.	本	běn	量 (mw)	*measure word*
9.	书	shū	名 (n.)	book
10.	桌子	zhuōzi	名 (n.)	desk
11.	支	zhī	量 (mw)	*measure word*
12.	笔	bǐ	名 (n.)	pen
13.	知道	zhīdào	动 (v.)	know
14.	现在	xiànzài	名 (n.)	now
15.	没	méi	副 (adv.)	no
16.	钱	qián	名 (n.)	money
17.	可以	kěyǐ	助动 (auxil. v.)	can
18.	别人	biéren	名 (n.)	other people
19.	附近	fùjìn	名 (n.)	neighborhood
20.	第一	dì yī		first
	第	dì	头 (pref.)	prefix for ordinal numbers
21.	路口	lùkǒu	名 (n.)	crossroad
22.	往	wǎng	动、介 (v./prep.)	head; to
23.	右	yòu	名 (n.)	right
24.	拐	guǎi	动 (v.)	turn
25.	红绿灯	hónglǜdēng	名 (n.)	traffic light
26.	就	jiù	副 (adv.)	just
27.	再	zài	副 (adv.)	again

Lesson Three Excuse me, is there a bank nearby?

28. 旁边　　　　pángbiān　　　名 (n.)　　　　　side, next to

Annotations

1. 个　　gè

"Gè" is one of the most frequently used measure word. It indicates a single person or thing. For example:

一个朋友	a friend		
这个东西	this thing	那个地方	that place
这个美国人	this American	那个学生	that student

2. 有　　yǒu

"Yǒu" is a verb that indicates possession or the existence of something. Its negative form is "méiyǒu". For example:

包里有什么？
What are the things in the bag?
这儿有超市吗？
Is there a supermarket near here?
这个路口没有红绿灯。
There isn't a traffic light at this corssroad.
我有几个中国朋友。
I have some Chinese friends.

Chinese Crash Course

3. 就　　*jiù*

The adverb "*jiù*" can indicate emphasis and assurance. For example:

就是那个地方。

It's just that place.

他就是李明。

He is Li Ming indeed.

银行就在超市附近。

The bank is just near the supermarket.

 **Exercises**

一　完成句子　Complete the following sentences.

1. A：你们学校附近有超市吗？

   B：(　　　　　)。

2. A：桌子上有(　　　　　)？

   B：有一支(　　　)和(　　　　)。

3. 银行就(　　　　)的前边，往右拐就是。

二　选择　Choose the correct answers.

1. 这儿前面(　)银行吗？

   A 在　　　　B 就　　　　C 有　　　　D 往

2. 桌子上有一(　)照相机。

   A 本　　　　B 支　　　　C 个　　　　D 的

Lesson Three Excuse me, is there a bank nearby?

3. 那个包里(　　)汉语课本。

   A 都有　　　　B 没有　　　　C 不有　　　　D 有没

三　选词填空　Fill in the following blanks with the proper words.

就　　　　知道　　　　旁边　　　　拐

1. 我(　　)李明在哪儿。

2. 超市(　　)有一个银行。

3. 照相机(　　)在桌子上。

4. 走到红绿灯往右(　　)就是网吧。

Supplementary Words

1. 一直	yìzhí	副 (adv.)	straight
2. 宾馆	bīnguǎn	名 (n.)	hotel
3. 怎么	zěnme	代 (pron.)	how
4. 走	zǒu	动 (v.)	walk
5. 左	zuǒ	名 (n.)	left
6. 座	zuò	量 (mw)	seat
7. 楼	lóu	名 (n.)	building
8. 向	xiàng	介 (prep.)	to
9. 北	běi	名 (n.)	north
10. 米	mǐ	量 (mw)	meter

Chinese Crash Course

11. 东	dōng	名 (n.)		east
12. 对不起	duìbuqǐ	动 (v.)		be sorry

Related Sentences

1. 这儿没有书店。
   Zhèr méiyǒu shūdiàn.
   There's no bookstore near here.

2. 请问,和平宾馆怎么走?
   Qǐngwèn, Hépíng Bīnguǎn zěnme zǒu?
   Excuse me, how can I get to Heping Hotel?

3. 一直往前走,再左拐就到了。
   Yìzhí wǎng qián zǒu, zài zuǒ guǎi jiù dào le.
   Go ahead, then turn left. It is just there.

4. 书店就在那座楼的后面。
   Shūdiàn jiù zài nà zuò lóu de hòumian.
   The bookstore is just behind that building.

5. 向北走100米,再向东拐。
   Xiàng běi zǒu yìbǎi mǐ, zài xiàng dōng guǎi.
   Walk 100 metres north, and then turn east.

6. 对不起,我也不知道。
   Duìbuqǐ, wǒ yě bù zhīdào.
   Sorry, I don't know either.

Dì Sì Kè Wǒmen de shēnghuó hěn xìngfú!
第4课 我们的生活很幸福！
Lesson Four　We lead a happy life!

Sentence Patterns

Tā shì wǒ gēge, yǐjīng jiéhūn le.
1. 他是我哥哥，已经结婚了。

He is my elder brother, and he is married.

Wǒ ài tāmen.
2. 我爱他们。

I love them.

Wǒmen de shēnghuó hěn xìngfú.
3. 我们的生活很幸福。

We lead a happy life.

Wǒmen liàn'ài liǎng nián le.
4. 我们恋爱两年了。

We have been in love for two years.

Wǒmen xiǎng míngnián jiéhūn.
5. 我们想明年结婚。

We plan to get married next year.

Wǒ yǐqián yǒu ge nǚpéngyou, kěshì fēnshǒu le.
6. 我以前有个女朋友，可是分手了。

I had a girlfriend before, but we said goodbye to each other.

Chinese Crash Course

    Wǒ xiǎng zhǎo ge Zhōngguó gūniang jiéhūn.
7. 我 想 找 个 中 国 姑 娘 结 婚。

I want to marry a Chinese girl.

    Kěyǐ kàn nǐ de zhàopiàn ma?
A：可 以 看 你 的 照 片 吗？

May I look at your photos?

    Dāngrán kěyǐ!
B：当 然 可 以！

Of course!

Lesson Four We lead a happy life!

A：Nǐmen jiā yǒu jǐ kǒu rén?
你们家有几口人？

How many people are there in your family?

B：Wǒmen yì jiā wǔ kǒu rén. Zhè shì wǒ de bàba, zhè shì wǒ māma hé mèimei.
我们一家五口人。这是我的爸爸，这是我妈妈和妹妹。

There are five people in my family. This is my father, this is my mother and this is my sister.

A：Tā shì nǐ gēge ba?
他是你哥哥吧？

Is he your elder brother?

B：Duì. Tā shì wǒ gēge, yǐjīng jiéhūn le.
对。他是我哥哥，已经结婚了。

Yes, he is my elder brother. He has got married.

A：Nǐmen de shēnghuó hěn xìngfú ba?
你们的生活很幸福吧？

Do you live a happy life?

B：Duì, wǒ ài tāmen.
对，我爱他们。

Yes, I love them.

A：Nàge nǚhái shì nǐ de nǚpéngyou ba?
那个女孩是你的女朋友吧？

Is that girl your girlfriend?

Chinese Crash Course

Shì, wǒmen liàn'ài yǐjīng liǎng nián le.
B：是，我们恋爱已经两年了。

Yes, we have been in love for two years.

Tā zhēn piàoliang!
A：她真漂亮！

How pretty she is!

Xièxie. Wǒmen xiǎng míngnián jiéhūn. Nǐ ne?
B：谢谢。我们想明年结婚。你呢？

Thank you. We plan to get married next year. What about you?

Wǒ yǐqián yǒu ge nǚpéngyou, kěshì fēnshǒu le.
A：我以前有个女朋友，可是分手了。

I had a girlfriend before, but we have broken up.

Zài Zhōngguó zhǎo xīn de àiqíng ba.
B：在中国找新的爱情吧。

You may find your new love in China.

Lesson Four We lead a happy life!

A：Wǒ xiǎng zhǎo yí ge Zhōngguó gūniang jiéhūn.
　我 想 找 一 个 中 国 姑 娘 结 婚。

I want to marry a Chinese girl.

 **New Words**

1. 看	kàn	动	(v.)	look at
2. 照片(相片)	zhàopiàn (xiàngpiàn)	名	(n.)	picture, photo
3. 当然	dāngrán	副	(adv.)	certainly
4. 口	kǒu	量	(mw)	*measure word*
5. 爸爸	bàba	名	(n.)	father
6. 妈妈	māma	名	(n.)	mother
7. 妹妹	mèimei	名	(n.)	younger sister
8. 哥哥	gēge	名	(n.)	elder brother
9. 已经	yǐjīng	副	(adv.)	already
10. 结婚	jié//hūn	动	(v.)	marry
11. 生活	shēnghuó	名、动	(n./v.)	life; live
12. 幸福	xìngfú	形	(adj.)	happy
13. 爱	ài	动	(v.)	love
14. 女孩	nǚhái	名	(n.)	girl
女	nǚ	名	(n.)	woman
15. 女朋友	nǚpéngyou	名	(n.)	girlfriend

Chinese Crash Course

16.	恋爱	liàn'ài	动 (v.)	fall in love
17.	两	liǎng	数 (num.)	two
18.	年	nián	名 (n.)	year
19.	了	le	助 (part.)	*particle*
20.	真	zhēn	副 (adv.)	really
21.	漂亮	piàoliang	形 (adj.)	beautiful, pretty
22.	明年	míngnián	名 (n.)	next year
23.	以前	yǐqián	名 (n.)	before
24.	可是	kěshì	连 (conj.)	but
25.	分手	fēn//shǒu	动 (v.)	part
26.	找	zhǎo	动 (v.)	find
27.	新	xīn	形 (adj.)	new
28.	爱情	àiqíng	名 (n.)	love
29.	姑娘	gūniang	名 (n.)	girl

Annotations

1. 可以　　kěyǐ

The optative verb "kěyǐ" indicates "permission". It is a polite way to ask for permission for doing sth. in an interrogative sentence. For example:

我可以在这里吗？　　　　——　你可以在这里。

Can I stay here?　　　　　　　——　Yes, you can stay here.

Lesson Four We lead a happy life!

我可以看你的词典吗？ —— 你可以看我的词典。

Can I use your dictionary? —— Yes, you can.

我可以看你的电脑吗？ —— 你可以看我的电脑。

Can I take a look at your computer? —— Yes, you can.

When answering questions, we can use "kěyǐ", "hǎo" or "dāngrán kěyǐ", but generally we do not use "bù kěyǐ".

2. 几　　jǐ

"Jǐ" refers to a number within ten in a question. For example:

你有几个中国朋友？

How many Chinese friends do you have?

你家有几口人？

How many people are there in your family?

包里有几本书？

How many books are there in the bag?

3. 吧　　ba

Auxiliary word "ba" is put at the end of a question. Its tone is lighter than "ma". The speaker already knows the answer but he or she wants to make sure. The falling tone is used at the end of the sentence. For example:

你是英国人吧？

Are you British?

她是你的女朋友吧？

Is she your girlfriend?

"Ba" also indicates the tone of suggestion, begging, encouragement or agreement. For example:

我们去吃饭吧!

Let's go to have dinner!

想爱你就去爱吧!

Go to love if you want to!

4. 很　　*hěn*

The adverb "*hěn*" indicates a high degree. For example:

我很爱她。

I love her very much.

认识你很高兴。

I'm very glad to meet you.

Generally "*hěn*" will be put before an adjectival-predicate. For example:

东西很多。(don't say "东西多")

There is a lot of stuff.

他很客气。(don't say "他客气")

He is very polite.

她很漂亮。(don't say "她漂亮")

She is very pretty.

5. 我的爸爸 / 我妈妈　　*wǒ de bàba / wǒ māma*

The auxiliary word "*de*" can be either used or omitted, when it is

Lesson Four We lead a happy life!

behind a single personal pronoun and followed by a noun which indicates kindred.

我爸爸	——	我的爸爸	my father
他的妻子	——	他妻子	his wife
他妹妹	——	他的妹妹	his younger sister
你儿子	——	你的儿子	your son

6. 了   *le*

The modal particle "le" can indicate the change of state when used at the end of a sentence. It also can indicate the affirmative mood.

我现在没有钱了。

I have no money now.

他已经结婚了。

He has got married.

我们谈恋爱两年了。

We have been in love for two years.

我们分手了。

We have broken up.

7. The capitalized forms of numbers 0 to 10 in Chinese are: "零, 一, 二, 三, 四, 五, 六, 七, 八, 九, 十". "Liǎng" and "èr" both mean two, "èr" is used in formal writing, while "liǎng" is combined with the measure word. We can't say "èr diànnǎo", "èr lǎoshī" and "èr nián". We can only say "liǎng tái diànnǎo", "liǎng wèi lǎoshī" and "liǎng nián".

Chinese Crash Course

 **Exercises**

一 完成句子 Complete the following sentences.

1. A：可以看你的电脑吗？
   B：(   )。

2. A：这个(   )吗？
   B：她不是我女朋友，是我妹妹。

3. A：你家有几口人？
   B：(   )。

二 选择 Choose the correct answers.

1. 我(   )看你的照片吗？
   A 是   B 对   C 想   D 可以

2. 我哥哥(   )结婚了。
   A 再   B 没   C 已经   D 就

3. (   )年以前我就有女朋友了。
   A 二   B 两   C 两个   D 二个

三 选词填空 Fill in the blanks with the proper words.

　　已经　　以前　　新　　找

1. 在中国我有了(   )的生活。
2. 我(   )没有女朋友了。
3. 我想(   )两个中国朋友。
4. 几年(   )我们已经认识了。

Lesson Four We lead a happy life!

Supplementary Words

1.	妻子	qīzi	名 (n.)	wife
2.	儿子	érzi	名 (n.)	son
3.	女儿	nǚ'ér	名 (n.)	daughter
4.	孩子	háizi	名 (n.)	child
5.	后来	hòulái	名 (n.)	later
6.	以后	yǐhòu	名 (n.)	after
7.	离婚	lí//hūn	动 (v.)	divorce
8.	男朋友	nánpéngyou	名 (n.)	boyfriend
9.	丈夫	zhàngfu	名 (n.)	husband
10.	快乐	kuàilè	形 (adj.)	happy

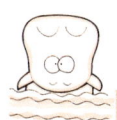

Related Sentences

1. 她是王老师的妻子。
   Tā shì Wáng lǎoshī de qīzi.
   She is Teacher Wang's wife.
2. 他们有一个儿子和一个女儿。
   Tāmen yǒu yí ge érzi hé yí ge nǚ'ér.
   They have a son and a daughter.

Chinese Crash Course

3. 我结婚以后不想要孩子。

    Wǒ jiéhūn yǐhòu bù xiǎng yào háizi.

    I don't want to have a baby after marriage.

4. 他们后来离婚了。

    Tāmen hòulái líhūn le.

    They divorced later.

5. 她又找了新男朋友。

    Tā yòu zhǎole xīn nánpéngyou.

    She has a new boyfriend again.

6. 她很爱她的丈夫。

    Tā hěn ài tā de zhàngfu.

    She loves her husband very much.

7. 他们很快乐。

    Tāmen hěn kuàilè.

    They're very happy.

Dì Wǔ Kè　Xiànzài jǐ diǎn le?
第 5 课 现在几点了？

Lesson Five　What time is it?

Sentence Patterns

Xiànzài jǐ diǎn le?
1. 现在几点了？

   What time is it?

   Chà yí kè shíyī diǎn.
2. 差一刻十一点。

   It is a quarter to eleven.

   Shíjiān guòde zhēn kuài!
3. 时间过得真快！

   Time goes so fast!

   Míngtiān nǐ jǐ diǎnzhōng qǐchuáng?
4. 明天你几点钟起床？

   When will you get up tomorrow morning?

   Láibují.
5. 来不及。

   It's too late.

   Shàngkè láidejí.
6. 上课来得及。

   There's still time to go to the class.

Chinese Crash Course

7. Jīntiān jǐ hào?
   今天几号？
   What's the date today?

8. Jīntiān xīngqī jǐ?
   今天星期几？
   What day is it today?

9. Jīntiān liù hào, xīngqīsān.
   今天6号，星期三。
   Today is 6th, Wednesday.

10. Kāi ge shēngrì wǎnhuì ba!
    开个生日晚会吧！
    Let's have a birthday party!

11. Tài hǎo le!
    太好了！
    That's great!

12. Wǒmen zhǔnbèi yíxià.
    我们准备一下。
    Let's get ready!

Dialogues

A: Dàwèi, xiànzài jǐ diǎn le?
大卫，现在几点了？
What time is it, David?

Lesson Five What time is it?

B: Chà yí kè shíyī diǎn.
差 一 刻 十 一 点。

It's a quarter to eleven.

A: Shíjiān guòde zhēn kuài.
时 间 过 得 真 快。

Time flies.

B: Míngtiān nǐ jǐ diǎnzhōng qǐchuáng?
明 天 你 几 点 钟 起 床?

When will you get up tomorrow morning?

A: Wǒ bā diǎn yǒu shì, wǒ xiǎng liù diǎn bàn zuǒyòu qǐchuáng.
我 八 点 有 事, 我 想 六 点 半 左 右 起 床。

I want to get up at about half past six. I have things to do at eight.

Chinese Crash Course

Wǒ bā diǎn èrshí qǐchuáng, jiǔ diǎn shàngkè.
B：我八点二十起床，九点上课。

I usually get up at twenty past eight. I will go to class at nine.

Láibují ba, huì chídào de.
A：来不及吧，会迟到的。

Maybe there's not enough time. You will be late.

Láidejí.
B：来得及。

There's still time.

Shí diǎn guò shí fēn le.
A：十点过十分了。

It's ten past ten.

Gāi xiūxi yíhuìr le.
B：该休息一会儿了。

It's time to have a break.

Jīntiān shì jǐ hào?
A：今天是几号？

What's the date today?

Jīntiān èrshísān hào.
B：今天 23 号。

Today is 23th.

Lesson Five What time is it?

A: Hòutiān shì wǒ de shēngrì.
后天是我的生日。

The day after tomorrow is my birthday.

B: Hòutiān xīngqī jǐ?
后天星期几?

What day is the day after tomorrow?

A: Jīntiān xīngqīwǔ, hòutiān shì xīngqītiān.
今天星期五,后天是星期天。

Today is Friday and the day after tomorrow would be Sunday.

B: Xīngqītiān wǒmen qīngsōng yíxià, kāi ge shēngrì wǎnhuì ba?
星期天我们轻松一下,开个生日晚会吧?

Let's relax on Sunday. How about having a birthday evening party?

Chinese Crash Course

　　　Tài hǎo le!
A：太 好 了！

Great!

　　　Nà wǒmen xīngqīliù zhǔnbèi yíxià.
B：那 我 们 星 期 六 准 备 一 下。

Then we will do some preparations on Saturday.

New Words

1. 点/点钟	diǎn/diǎnzhōng	量 (mw)	o'clock
2. 差	chà	动、形 (v./adj.)	fall short of; inferior
3. 刻	kè	量 (mw)	quarter
4. 时间	shíjiān	名 (n.)	time
5. 快	kuài	形 (adj.)	quick
6. 明天	míngtiān	名 (n.)	tomorrow
7. 起床	qǐ//chuáng	动 (v.)	get up
8. 八	bā	数 (num.)	eight
9. 事	shì	名 (n.)	thing
10. 六	liù	数 (num.)	six
11. 半	bàn	形 (adj.)	half
12. 左右	zuǒyòu	名 (n.)	about
13. 二十	èrshí	数 (num.)	twenty

Lesson Five   What time is it?

14. 九	jiǔ	数 (num.)		nine
15. 上课	shàng//kè	动 (v.)		attend class
16. 来不及	láibují	动 (v.)		it's too late
17. 会	huì	动、助动 (v./auxil. v.)		can
18. 迟到	chídào	动 (v.)		be late
19. 来得及	láidejí	动 (v.)		there's still time
20. 十	shí	数 (num.)		ten
21. 过	guò	动 (v.)		pass
22. 分/分钟	fēn/fēnzhōng	量 (mw)		minute
23. 该/应该	gāi/yīnggāi	助动 (auxil. v.)		should
24. 休息	xiūxi	动 (v.)		rest, have a break
25. 一会儿	yíhuìr	数量 (num.-class.)		for a while (numeral-classifier compound)
26. 今天	jīntiān	名 (n.)		today
27. 号	hào	名 (n.)		date
28. 后天	hòutiān	名 (n.)		the day after tomorrow
29. 生日	shēngrì	名 (n.)		birthday
30. 星期	xīngqī	名 (n.)		week
31. 星期天/星期日	xīngqītiān/xīngqīrì	名 (n.)		Sunday
32. 轻松	qīngsōng	形 (adj.)		relaxed
33. 开	kāi	动 (v.)		have

Chinese Crash Course

34.	晚会	wǎnhuì	名 (n.)	evening party
35.	太	tài	副 (adv.)	too
36.	准备	zhǔnbèi	动 (v.)	prepare

Annotations

1. 时间表达法　　*shíjiān biǎodáfǎ*

Fifteen minutes is a quarter. "*Chà yí kè*" means a quarter to and "*guò yí kè*" means a quarter past. Two o'clock sharp can be said as "*liǎng diǎn zhěng*" or "*zhěng liǎng diǎn*". For example:

三点钟、三点、整三点、三点整	(3:00)
三点过五分、三点零五分	(3:05)
三点一刻、三点过一刻、三点十五、三点十五分	(3:15)
三点半	(3:30)
三点四十五、三点四十五分、三点三刻、差一刻四点	(3:45)
三点五十八分、三点五十八、差两分四点	(3:58)

2. When you ask or answer the date or time, the verb "*shì*" can be omitted.

今天(是)几号？　　——　　今天(是)6号。
What date is it today?　——　Today is 6th.
现在(是)7点。
It's 7 o'clock.

Lesson Five What time is it?

明天星期几?　　　　——　　明天(是)星期日。
What day is tomorrow?　——　　Tomorrow is Sunday.

3. **真**　　*zhēn*

   The adverb "*zhēn*" is used for emphasis with the meaning of "*quèshí*" or "*shízài*". For example:

   他们真幸福!
   How happy they are!
   你真漂亮!
   How beautiful you are!
   他真是个好人!
   He is such a good man!

4. **轻松一下**　　*qīngsōng yíxià*

   Verbs of single syllable can be used in structures like "V+*yī*+V", "VV" or "V *yíxià*" which indicates the action is quick or the degree is light. For example:

看一看照片	看看照片	看一下照片	look at the photo
找一找	找找	找一下	look for
想一想	想想	想一下	think about

   Dissyllabic verbs can be followed by "*yíxià*" or used in the pattern "ABAB". For example:

   | 轻松一下 | 轻松轻松 | have a relaxation |
   | 准备一下 | 准备准备 | make a preparation |

Chinese Crash Course

5. 好   hǎo

"Hǎo" can indicate agreement and assent. For example:

A：你也来吧。

　　Come with us.

B：好。

　　OK.

6. 太好了！   Tài hǎo le!

"Tài+ adjective + le" is a fixed form. It indicates the degree is very high. For example:

那个女孩太漂亮了！

That girl is so pretty!

您太客气了！

You are so polite!

这个电脑太大了！

This computer is too big!

7. "一"的变调   "yī" de biàndiào

The tone of "yī" is the first tone. When it is followed by a first, second, or a third tone word, you should pronounce it as the fourth tone. For example:

找一找	zhǎo yì zhǎo	look for
等一等	děng yì děng	wait for

It is pronounced as the second tone when it is followed by a fourth

Lesson Five What time is it?

tone word. For example:

| 一个 | yí ge | one |
| 看一看 | kàn yí kàn | look at |

 **Exercises**

一 完成句子 Complete the following sentences.

1. A：现在几点了？
   B：(　　　　　)。

2. A：明天你(　　　　)起床？
   B：六点半。

3. A：你们几点上课？
   B：(　　　　　)。

4. A：今天是几号？星期几？
   B：(　　　　)，(　　　　　)。

5. A：今天开个晚会怎么样？
   B：(　　　　)，(　　　　　　)。

二 选择 Choose the correct answers.

1. 我想(　　　　　)。
   A 明天六点起床　　B 六点起床明天
   C 起床明天六点　　D 六点明天起床

2. 我的生日晚会是(　　　　　)。
   A 这个星期七　　B 这个5号
   C 这个星期日　　D 星期天这个

Chinese Crash Course

3. 今天我们(　　　　)。

　　A 一下轻松　　B 轻松　　C 轻轻松松　　D 轻松一下

三　请读出下列时间　Please read the times given below aloud.

　　7:45　　　8:30　　　11:11　　　23:05　　　10:50

Supplementary Words

1. 月	yuè	名 (n.)	month
2. 周末	zhōumò	名 (n.)	weekend
3. 月末	yuèmò	名 (n.)	end of the month
4. 年末	niánmò	名 (n.)	end of the year
5. 中午	zhōngwǔ	名 (n.)	noon
6. 上个月	shàng ge yuè		last month
7. 下个月	xià ge yuè		next month

Related Sentences

1. 他出生于1989年6月23日。
   Tā chūshēng yú yījiǔbājiǔ nián liù yuè èrshísān rì.
   He was born on June 23th, 1989.

Lesson Five　What time is it?

2. 这个周末有时间吗？

   Zhège zhōumò yǒu shíjiān ma?

   Do you have time this weekend?

3. 我周六有空儿。

   Wǒ zhōuliù yǒu kòngr.

   I have time on Saturday.

4. 周末愉快！

   Zhōumò yúkuài!

   Have a nice weekend!

5. 这个周末我没有事。

   Zhège zhōumò wǒ méiyǒu shì.

   I'm free this weekend.

Dì Liù Kè Míngtiān wǎnshang nǐ yǒu shíjiān ma?
第 6 课 明天晚上你有时间吗？
Lesson Six Do you have time tomorrow evening?

 **Sentence Patterns**

Nǐ zuìjìn zěnmeyàng?
1. 你最近怎么样？

   How are you getting on?

   Wǒ zuìjìn hěn máng.
2. 我最近很忙。

   I have been very busy recently.

   Wǒ juéde hěn yǒu yìsi.
3. 我觉得很有意思。

   I feel it is very interesting.

   Wǒ hěn xǐhuan zhèli de shēnghuó.
4. 我很喜欢这里的生活。

   I like the life here very much.

   Tā shénme shíhou lái Zhōngguó?
5. 她什么时候来中国？

   When will she come to China?

   Zuótiān xiàwǔ nǐ qù nǎr le?
6. 昨天下午你去哪儿了？

   Where did you go yesterday afternoon?

Lesson Six Do you have time tomorrow evening?

7. Míngtiān wǎnshang nǐ yǒu shíjiān ma?
明天晚上你有时间吗?

Do you have time tomorrow evening?

8. Wǒ qǐng nǐmen chī fàn.
我请你们吃饭。

I invite you to dinner.

9. Méi wèntí.
没问题。

No problem.

10. Míngtiān wǎnshang jiàn.
明天晚上见。

See you tomorrow evening.

 **Dialogues**

A: Àimǎ, zuìjìn zěnmeyàng?
艾玛,最近怎么样?

How are you getting on, Emma?

B: Zuìjìn hěn máng, dànshì wǒ juéde hěn yǒu yìsi.
最近很忙,但是我觉得很有意思。

I have been very busy, but I feel it is very interesting.

Chinese Crash Course

A: <ruby>我<rt>Wǒ</rt></ruby> <ruby>也<rt>yě</rt></ruby> <ruby>喜欢<rt>xǐhuan</rt></ruby> <ruby>这里<rt>zhèli</rt></ruby> <ruby>的<rt>de</rt></ruby> <ruby>生活<rt>shēnghuó</rt></ruby>。

I also like the life here.

B: <ruby>你<rt>Nǐ</rt></ruby> <ruby>的<rt>de</rt></ruby> <ruby>女朋友<rt>nǚpéngyou</rt></ruby> <ruby>什么<rt>shénme</rt></ruby> <ruby>时候<rt>shíhou</rt></ruby> <ruby>来<rt>lái</rt></ruby> <ruby>中国<rt>Zhōngguó</rt></ruby>?

When will your girlfriend come to China?

A: <ruby>下<rt>Xià</rt></ruby> <ruby>个<rt>ge</rt></ruby> <ruby>星期<rt>xīngqī</rt></ruby> <ruby>到<rt>dào</rt></ruby> <ruby>北京<rt>Běijīng</rt></ruby>。

She will be in Beijing next week.

B: <ruby>太<rt>Tài</rt></ruby> <ruby>好<rt>hǎo</rt></ruby> <ruby>了<rt>le</rt></ruby>! <ruby>你们<rt>Nǐmen</rt></ruby> <ruby>就<rt>jiù</rt></ruby> <ruby>要<rt>yào</rt></ruby> <ruby>见面<rt>jiànmiàn</rt></ruby> <ruby>了<rt>le</rt></ruby>。

That's great! You will see each other soon.

Lesson Six Do you have time tomorrow evening?

Dàwèi, zuìjìn hǎo ma?
A：大卫，最近好吗？

How are you getting on, David?

Hái kěyǐ.
B：还可以。

I'm OK.

Zuótiān xiàwǔ nǐ qù nǎr le?
A：昨天下午你去哪儿了？

Where did you go yesterday afternoon?

B：*Wǒ hé Zhōngguó péngyou qù túshūguǎn le.*
我和中国朋友去图书馆了。

I went to the library with my Chinese friends.

A：*Míngtiān wǎnshang nǐ yǒu shíjiān ma?*
明天晚上你有时间吗？

Are you free tomorrow evening?

B：*Yǒu shì ma?*
有事吗？

Anything I can do for you?

A：*Wǒ xiǎng qǐng nǐmen chī fàn, zěnmeyàng?*
我想请你们吃饭，怎么样？

I want to invite you to dinner. Is it OK for you?

B：*Hǎo a! Wèi shénme qǐng wǒmen?*
好啊！为什么请我们？

Good! But what for?

A：*Míngtiān shì wǒ de shēngrì.*
明天是我的生日。

Tomorrow is my birthday.

B：*Tài hǎo le! Míngtiān jǐ diǎn? Zài shénme dìfang?*
太好了！明天几点？在什么地方？

That's great! At what time tomorrow and which place?

A：*Wǎnshang liù diǎn bàn, zài "Hǎo Shēnghuó Fàndiàn".*
晚上六点半，在"好生活饭店"。

Half past six in the evening at "Good Life Restaurant".

B：*Méi wèntí! Míngtiān wǎnshang jiàn.*
没问题！明天晚上见。

No problem! See you tomorrow evening.

Lesson Six Do you have time tomorrow evening?

New Words

1.	最近	zuìjìn	名 (n.)	recentness
2.	怎么样	zěnmeyàng	代 (pron.)	how about
3.	忙	máng	形、动 (adj./v.)	busy; be busy with
4.	但是	dànshì	连 (conj.)	but
5.	觉得	juéde	动 (v.)	feel
6.	有意思	yǒu yìsi		interesting
7.	喜欢	xǐhuan	动 (v.)	like
8.	时候	shíhou	名 (n.)	time
9.	到	dào	动 (v.)	arrive
10.	下	xià	名 (n.)	next
11.	要……了	yào……le		be about to
12.	见面	jiàn//miàn	动 (v.)	meet
13.	昨天	zuótiān	名 (n.)	yesterday
14.	下午	xiàwǔ	名 (n.)	afternoon
15.	朋友	péngyou	名 (n.)	friend
16.	晚上	wǎnshang	名 (n.)	evening
17.	啊	a	助 (part.)	*particle*
18.	为什么	wèi shénme		why

Chinese Crash Course

19. 没问题	méi wèntí		no problem
问题	wèntí	名 (n.)	problem
20. 见	jiàn	动 (v.)	meet

Proper Noun

北京　　　　Běijīng　　　　　　　Beijing

Annotations

1. 最近怎么样？/最近好吗？　　Zuìjìn zěnmeyàng? / Zuìjìn hǎo ma?

The two sentences are used for greeting people. "Zěnmeyàng" is not used to get opinions, and is used just to ask the condition or state of sb.. If it's not good, you can answer "bù zěnmeyàng". For example:

A：最近怎么样？

　　How are you getting on?

B：很好！/不怎么样。

　　Very well! /Not good.

2. 但是　　dànshì

The conjunction "dànshì" indicates transition. For example:

Lesson Six Do you have time tomorrow evening?

那个饭店以前不好,但是最近很好。

That restaurant wasn't good before, but it has been nice recently.

她很漂亮,但是我不喜欢她。

She is very beautiful, but I don't like her.

那个笔记本电脑很好,但是很大。

That laptop computer is very good, but it is too big.

3. 时间词做状语　shíjiān cí zuò zhuàngyǔ

A temporal word can serve as an adverbial. It indicates the time that an action or a state happens and is put before the predicate.

你妹妹什么时候去美国?

When will your little sister go to the United States?

明天你几点起床?

When will you get up tomorrow?

我八点上课。

The class begins at eight o'clock.

昨天晚上你去哪儿了?

Where did you go yesterday evening?

4. 怎么样　zěnmeyàng

"Zěnmeyàng" can be used for asking opinion. "Bù zěnmeyàng" is a negative answer.

我们开个晚会怎么样?

How about we have an evening party?

我们去吃饭怎么样?

How about we go for dinner?

5. 就要……了 *jiùyào……le*

"Yào……le" indicates that something will happen. When the adverb "jiù" is added before "yào", it indicates sth. is going to happen immediately.

就要上课了。

Class is to begin in no time.

晚会就要开始了。

The evening party is going to start.

6. 你去哪儿了? *Nǐ qù nǎr le?*

"Le" is put after the verb or at the end of a sentence to indicate an action has been done. For example:

昨天我去了网吧。

I went to the internet cafe yesterday.

星期一你去了哪儿?

Where did you go Monday?

李老师来了吗?

Has Teacher Li been here?

昨晚他们开了晚会。

They held an evening party last night.

7. 为什么 *wèi shénme*

It is used to ask for the reason. For example:

艾玛为什么来中国?

Why does Emma come to China?

Lesson Six　Do you have time tomorrow evening?

他们为什么开晚会？
Why did they hold the evening party?
他为什么不喜欢中国菜？
Why doesn't he like Chinese food?

Exercises

 完成句子　Complete the following sentences.

1. A：你最近的生活怎么样？
   B：(　　　　　)。

2. A：你昨天去哪儿了？
   B：(　　　　　)。

3. A：你们什么时候考试？
   B：(　　　　　)。

4. A：你明天想请谁吃饭？
   B：(　　　　　)。

5. A：你最近有时间去玩吗？为什么？
   B：(　　　　)，(　　　　　)。

 选择　Choose the correct answers.

1. 大卫：昨天的晚会怎么样？
   艾玛：(　　　　　)。

   A 不有意思　　　　B 非常很好

Chinese Crash Course

　　C 不怎么样　　　　　　D 太好
2. 明天晚上我(　　)你们吃饭。
　　A 请问　　　　　　　　B 请看
　　C 去　　　　　　　　　D 请
3. 她妈妈(　　　　)来中国了。
　　A 要　　　　　　　　　B 什么时候
　　C 怎么样　　　　　　　D 太
4. 晚上六点半(　　　　)。
　　A 见面我们　　　　　　B 我们见面
　　C 就我们见面　　　　　D 见面我们了
5. 昨天下午我们去网吧(　　)。
　　A 呢　　　　　　　　　B 吗
　　C 了　　　　　　　　　D 哪儿

三　选词填空　Fill in the blanks with the proper words.

　　忙　　来　　去　　时间　　为什么　　生活

1. 我最近的(　　)非常好。
2. 下午你(　　)哪儿了？
3. 明天你(　　)我这里吗？
4. 她今天很(　　)吗？
5. 你们星期天有(　　)吗？
6. 她(　　)不吃饭？

Lesson Six Do you have time tomorrow evening?

Supplementary Words

1. 没(有)意思	méi(yǒu) yìsi		not interesting
2. 上午	shàngwǔ	名 (n.)	morning
3. 一般	yìbān	形、副 (adj./adv.)	general; generally
4. 老地方	lǎo dìfang		old place
5. 老样子	lǎo yàngzi		same as usual
6. 约会	yuēhuì	动、名 (v./n.)	date; date
7. 空儿	kòngr	名 (n.)	spare time

Related Sentences

1. 好久不见!

    Hǎojiǔ bú jiàn!

    Long time no see!

2. 上个星期我去看朋友了。

    Shàng ge xīngqī wǒ qù kàn péngyou le.

    I went to see my friends last week.

3. 不见不散!

    Bú jiàn bú sàn!

    Don't leave till we weet!

Chinese Crash Course

4. 我还是老样子。

   Wǒ hái shì lǎo yàngzi.

   I'm still the same as usual.

5. 明天有空儿吗?

   Míngtiān yǒu kòngr ma?

   Are you free tomorrow?

6. 明天下午四点,说好了。

   Míngtiān xiàwǔ sì diǎn, shuō hǎo le.

   At four tomorrow afternoon. It's a deal.

7. 这个晚会太没有意思了!

   Zhège wǎnhuì tài méiyǒu yìsi le!

   This evening party is too boring!

8. 最近不怎么样。

   Zuìjìn bù zěnmeyàng.

   I don't feel very well recently.

9. 没事了,我先走了。再见!

   Méi shì le, wǒ xiān zǒu le. Zàijiàn!

   Everything's done. I've got to go. Bye!

第 7 课 你要吃点儿什么？
Dì Qī Kè Nǐ yào chī diǎnr shénme?

Lesson Seven   What would you like to eat?

 **Sentence Patterns**

1. 我请你吃烤鸭吧。
   Wǒ qǐng nǐ chī kǎoyā ba.

   I invite you to eat roast duck.

2. 有一点儿油腻。
   Yǒu yìdiǎnr yóunì.

   It's a little greasy.

3. 这个菜一定适合您的口味。
   Zhège cài yídìng shìhé nín de kǒuwèi.

   The dish must suit your taste.

4. 这家餐厅环境不错。
   Zhè jiā cāntīng huánjìng búcuò.

   The environment of this restaurant is good.

5. 您要吃点儿什么？
   Nín yào chī diǎnr shénme?

   What would you like to eat?

6. 这是菜谱，请您点菜。
   Zhè shì càipǔ, qǐng nín diǎncài.

   Here is the menu. Please order.

Chinese Crash Course

7. Nín lái diǎnr shénme jiǔshuǐ hé yǐnliào?
   您来点儿什么酒水和饮料？

   What kind of wine and drink do you want?

8. Nín shāo děng, nín de cài hěn kuài jiù lái.
   您稍等，您的菜很快就来。

   Please wait for a moment. Your dish will be ready soon.

Dialogues

A: Wǒ è le, wǒ xiǎng chī Zhōngguócài.
我饿了，我想吃中国菜。

I'm hungry. I want to eat Chinese dish.

B: Wǒ qǐng nǐ chī kǎoyā ba.
我请你吃烤鸭吧。

Let me invite you to eat roast duck.

A: Kǎoyā yǒu yìdiǎnr yóunì.
烤鸭有一点儿油腻。

The roast duck is a little greasy.

B: Nà Sìchuān huǒguō zěnmeyàng?
那四川火锅怎么样？

How about Sichuan hot pot?

Lesson Seven What would you like to eat?

A: Tài là le, wǒ bù xíguàn.
太辣了，我不习惯。

It's too hot. I'm not used to it.

B: Hóngshāo páigǔ yídìng shìhé nǐ de kǒuwèi.
红烧排骨一定适合你的口味。

The pork ribs braised in soy sauce must suit your taste.

A: Hǎo, wǒ hái xiǎng chī miàntiáo.
好，我还想吃面条。

OK, I also like to eat noodles.

B: Wǒ zhīdao yì jiā cāntīng, huánjìng búcuò.
我知道一家餐厅，环境不错。

I know a restaurant with nice environment.

A: Cài hǎochī jiù kěyǐ, zǒu ba.
菜好吃就可以，走吧。

It is ok as long as the dish is delicious. Let's go.

Chinese Crash Course

A: Nín hǎo, nín yào chī diǎnr shénme?
您好，您要吃点儿什么？
Hello, what would you like to have?

B: Fúwùyuán, wǒmen diǎn ge hóngshāo páigǔ.
服务员，我们点个红烧排骨。
We'd like to have the pork ribs braised in soy sauce.

A: Hǎo de. Zhè shì càipǔ, nín hái yào shénme?
好的。这是菜谱，您还要什么？
OK. Here is the menu. Do you need anything else?

B: Zài lái yí ge shuǐzhǔyú ba.
再来一个水煮鱼吧。
We'd like to have a boiled spicy fish slices then.

Lesson Seven What would you like to eat?

A：Nà zhǔshí diǎn shénme?
那 主 食 点 什 么？

What do you like for principal food?

B：Lái yì jīn shuǐjiǎo ba.
来 一 斤 水 饺 吧。

We'd like to have half a kilogram of boiled dumplings.

A：Nín hē shénme jiǔshuǐ hé yǐnliào?
您 喝 什 么 酒 水 和 饮 料？

What wine and drink do you want?

B：Lái yì píng píjiǔ hé yì píng guǒzhī.
来 一 瓶 啤 酒 和 一 瓶 果 汁。

One bottle of beer and one bottle of fruit juice.

A：Nín shāo děng, nǐmen de cài hěn kuài jiù lái.
您 稍 等，你 们 的 菜 很 快 就 来。

A moment please. Your dish will be ready soon.

New Words

1. 饿	è	形 (adj.)	hungry
2. 中国菜	Zhōngguócài	名 (n.)	Chinese cuisine
3. 烤鸭	kǎoyā	名 (n.)	roast duck
4. 一点儿	yìdiǎnr	数量 (num.-class.)	a little
5. 火锅	huǒguō	名 (n.)	hot pot

Chinese Crash Course

6. 油腻	yóunì	形 (adj.)	greasy
7. 辣	là	形 (adj.)	hot, spicy
8. 习惯	xíguàn	名、动 (n./v.)	habit; get used to
9. 红烧排骨	hóngshāo páigǔ		pork ribs braised in soy sauce
10. 一定	yídìng	副 (adv.)	must
11. 适合	shìhé	动 (v.)	fit, suit
12. 口味	kǒuwèi	名 (n.)	taste
13. 还	hái	副 (adv.)	also, still
14. 面条	miàntiáo	名 (n.)	noodle
15. 餐厅	cāntīng	名 (n.)	restaurant
16. 环境	huánjìng	名 (n.)	environment
17. 不错	búcuò	形 (adj.)	good
18. 菜	cài	名 (n.)	dish
19. 好吃	hǎochī	形 (adj.)	delicious
20. 服务员	fúwùyuán	名 (n.)	waiter
21. 点	diǎn	动 (v.)	order
22. 菜谱	càipǔ	名 (n.)	menu
23. 水煮鱼	shuǐzhǔyú	名 (n.)	boiled spicy fish slices
24. 主食	zhǔshí	名 (n.)	staple food
25. 斤	jīn	量 (mw)	half a kilogram
26. 水饺/饺子	shuǐjiǎo/jiǎozi	名 (n.)	dumpling
27. 喝	hē	动 (v.)	drink

Lesson Seven   What would you like to eat?

28. 酒水	jiǔshuǐ	名 (n.)	beverages and alcohol
29. 饮料	yǐnliào	名 (n.)	drink
30. 瓶	píng	名、量 (n./mw)	bottle
31. 啤酒	píjiǔ	名 (n.)	beer
32. 果汁	guǒzhī	名 (n.)	fruit juice
33. 稍	shāo	副 (adv.)	a little
34. 等	děng	动 (v.)	wait

Proper Noun

四川   Sìchuān   Sichuan

Annotations

1. 一点儿   yìdiǎnr

"Yǒu yìdiǎnr" is used as an adverbial and it indicates dissatisfaction or a negative meaning. "Yì" can be omitted. For example:

那个电子词典有点儿大。

That electronic dictionary is a little big.

那个东西有点儿贵。

That thing is a little expensive.

现在有点儿忙,你再等一个小时。

I'm a little busy now. Please wait for another hour.

"Yìdiǎnr" can also be used as an attribute. For example:

您要吃点儿什么?

What would you like to have?

他吃了一点儿饭。

He has just eaten a little.

"Yìdiǎnr" is used as a complement to indicate suggestion, urgency or order. For example:

快点儿,要迟到了。

Hurry up. It's too late.

走慢点儿,我累了。

Please walk slowly. I'm tired.

再多点儿。

Please give me more.

2. 我不习惯　　**wǒ bù xíguàn**

"Xíguàn" can be a verb or a noun. For example:

我习惯了这里的生活。　　(动)

I have been accustomed to the life here.

每天6点起床,这是他的习惯。　(名)

Getting up at six o'clock every day is his habit.

Lesson Seven What would you like to eat?

3. 还　*hái*

The adverb "*hái*" indicates reluctance. For instance "*hái kěyǐ*". Here it means "also, again". For example:

我还点了一个凉菜。

I also ordered a cold dish.

我们还有一个小时的时间。

We still have an hour.

你还要什么？

What else would you like to have?

4. 这家餐厅/这家酒吧　*zhè jiā cāntīng / zhè jiā jiǔbā*

"Jiā" is a measure word for corporation or business. For example:

一家饭店　　　一家公司　　　一家网吧

a restaurant　　a corporation　　an internet cafe

 **Exercises**

一　完成句子　Complete the following sentences.

1. A：先生，您要点什么菜？

   B：(　　　　　)。

   A：对不起，我们的菜单没有四川菜。

   B：没问题，我(　　　　　)。

2. A：小姐，(　　　　　)？

B：我要青岛啤酒。

A：(　　　　)？

B：要三瓶。

二 选择　Choose the correct answers.

1. 我们点了(　　)菜。

　A 二　　　B 二个　　　C 两个　　　D 两

2. 四川菜很适合我的(　　　)。

　A 习惯　　B 口味　　　C 菜　　　　D 餐厅

3. 这个菜(　　)辣，我不习惯。

　A 一点儿　B 有点儿　　C 一点儿有　D 点儿

三 选词填空　Fill in the blanks with the proper words.

　　油腻　　　要　　　菜谱　　　　点

1. 这个菜太(　　)了。

2. 服务员，我要看看(　　　)。

3. 大卫(　　)了烤鸭，有点儿贵。

4. 你(　　)喝什么啤酒？

Lesson Seven   What would you like to eat?

Supplementary Words

1. 酒吧	jiǔbā	名 (n.)	bar
2. 西餐	xīcān	名 (n.)	Western food
3. 中餐	zhōngcān	名 (n.)	Chinese food
4. 面包	miànbāo	名 (n.)	bread
5. 包间/单间	bāojiān/dānjiān	名 (n.)	separate room (rented in a restaurant)
6. 蔬菜	shūcài	名 (n.)	vegetable
7. 凉菜	liángcài	名 (n.)	cold dish
8. 炒菜	chǎocài	名 (n.)	stir-fried dish
9. 特色菜	tèsècài	名 (n.)	special dish
10. 买单	mǎidān	动 (v.)	pay the bill
11. 算账	suàn//zhàng	动 (v.)	pay the bill
12. 请客	qǐng//kè	动 (v.)	invite somebody to dinner
13. 咸	xián	形 (adj.)	salty
14. 清淡	qīngdàn	形 (adj.)	light
15. 东北菜	Dōngběicài	名 (n.)	Northeastern cuisine
16. 湘菜	Xiāngcài	名 (n.)	Hunan cuisine
17. 粤菜	Yuècài	名 (n.)	Guangdong cuisine

Chinese Crash Course

18. 宫保鸡丁 gōngbǎojīdīng 名 (n.) sauted chicken cubes with chilli and peanuts

19. 鱼香肉丝 yúxiāngròusī 名 (n.) fish-flavored shredded pork

20. 糖醋鱼 tángcùyú 名 (n.) fish in sweet and sour sauce

Related Sentences

1. A: 晚上好！请问您几位？
   Wǎnshang hǎo! Qǐngwèn nín jǐ wèi?
   Good evening! How many in your group?

   B: 我们一共六位。
   Wǒmen yígòng liù wèi.
   There are totally six people.

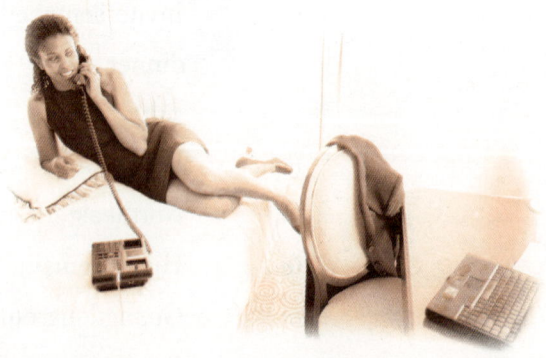

Lesson Seven   *What would you like to eat?*

A: 您订房间了吗?

Nín dìng fángjiān le ma?

Have you reserved any room?

B: 订了。我姓张。

Dìng le. Wǒ xìng Zhāng.

Yes, my surname is Zhang.

A: 您订的单间在二楼,请跟我来。

Nín dìng de dānjiān zài èr lóu, qǐng gēn wǒ lái.

Your room is at the second floor. Follow me, please.

2. 服务员,你们有什么特色菜?

Fúwùyuán, nǐmen yǒu shénme tèsècài?

What's your specialty here?

3. 你吃中餐还是西餐?

Nǐ chī zhōngcān háishi xīcān?

Which do you like, Chinese food or Western food?

Chinese Crash Course

4. 今天我来。/今天我请客。

   Jīntiān wǒ lái. / Jīntiān wǒ qǐngkè.

   It's my treat today.

5. 服务员,买单。

   Fúwùyuán, mǎidān.

   Waiter, I would like to pay the bill.

6. 一共是一百六十元,开发票吗?

   Yígòng shì yìbǎi liùshí yuán, kāi fāpiào ma?

   It is one hundred and sixty yuan. Do you want an invoice?

第8课 我现在上网看我的邮箱。
Dì Bā Kè Wǒ xiànzài shàngwǎng kàn wǒ de yóuxiāng.

Lesson Eight   I'm checking my mailbox on the internet.

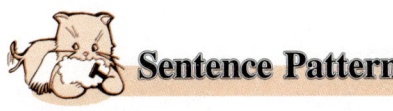

Sentence Patterns

1. 喂，请问刘涛在吗？
   Wèi, qǐngwèn Liú Tāo zài ma?
   Hello. May I speak to Liu Tao?

2. 我就是，您是哪位？
   Wǒ jiù shì, nín shì nǎ wèi?
   Speaking. Who's that speaking?

3. 我后天再给你打电话。
   Wǒ hòutiān zài gěi nǐ dǎ diànhuà.
   I will call you the day after tomorrow.

4. 我明天晚上等你电话。
   Wǒ míngtiān wǎnshang děng nǐ diànhuà.
   I will wait for your call tomorrow evening.

5. 我的手机号码是 13833789089。
   Wǒ de shǒujī hàomǎ shì 13833789089.
   My mobile phone number is 13833789089.

6. Shōudào wǒ de diànzǐ yóujiàn le ma?
收到我的电子邮件了吗？

Did you receive my e-mail?

7. Wǒ xiànzài shàngwǎng kàn yíxià.
我现在上网看一下。

I will check it at once.

8. Yěxǔ shì wǎngluò yǒu wèntí.
也许是网络有问题。

Maybe there is something wrong with the network.

9. Wǒ zài fā yí cì.
我再发一次。

I will send it to you again.

 **Dialogues**

A: Wèi, nǐ hǎo, qǐngwèn Liú Tāo xiānsheng zài ma?
喂，你好，请问刘涛先生在吗？

Hello. May I speak to Mr. Liu Tao?

B: Wǒ jiù shì, qǐngwèn nǐ shì nǎ wèi?
我就是，请问你是哪位？

This is Liu Tao speaking. Who's that?

Lesson Eight I'm checking my mailbox on the internet.

A: Liú xiānsheng, wǒ shì Wáng Hóng, zuótiān wǒmen tōngguo diànhuà.
刘先生，我是王红，昨天我们通过电话。

Mr. Liu, this is Wang Hong speaking. I called you yesterday.

B: Ò, gōngsī de gōngzuò hòutiān kāishǐ, wǒ hòutiān zài gěi nǐ dǎ diànhuà.
哦，公司的工作后天开始，我后天再给你打电话。

Yes. I will start working the day after tomorrow. I will call you then.

A: Hǎo de, nà hòutiān shàngwǔ wǒ děng nǐ de diànhuà.
好的，那后天上午我等你的电话。

OK. I'll wait for your call in the morning the day after tomorrow.

B: Kěyǐ gàosu wǒ nǐ de shǒujī hàomǎ ma? Zuótiān nǐ
可以告诉我你的手机号码吗？昨天你

de fángjiān diànhuà méi rén jiē.
的房间电话没人接。

Can you tell me your mobile phone number? Nobody answered the phone in your room yesterday.

A: Zuótiān wǒ chūqu le. Wǒ de shǒujī shì 13811184675.
昨天我出去了。我的手机是13811184675。

I was out yesterday. My mobile phone number is 13811184675.

B: 13811184675, hǎo, wǒ jìzhù le.
13811184675，好，我记住了。

13811184675. OK. I got it.

A: Nà máfan nǐ le.
那麻烦你了。

Well, sorry for troubling you.

B: Bú kèqi, zài liánxi.
不客气，再联系。

You are welcome. Get in touch next time.

A: Wèi, shì Àimǎ ma?
喂，是艾玛吗？

Hello. Is Emma speaking?

B: Shì wǒ. Nǐ shì Dàwèi ba?
是我。你是大卫吧？

Speaking. Is that David speaking?

Lesson Eight I'm checking my mailbox on the internet.

A: Duì. Nǐ shōudào wǒ fā de diànzǐ yóujiàn le ma?
对。你收到我发的电子邮件了吗？
Yes. Have you received my e-mail?

B: Shì shénme shíhou fā de?
是什么时候发的？
When did you send it?

A: Zuótiān wǎnshang fā de.
昨天晚上发的。
I sent it to you last night.

B: Wǒ xiànzài shàngwǎng kàn yíxià, shāo děng.
我现在上网看一下，稍等。
I'll check it at once. Wait for a moment.

(guòle yíhuìr)
(过了一会儿)

(after a while)

Chinese Crash Course

B: Wèi, Dàwèi, wǒ hái méiyou shōudào yóujiàn.
喂，大卫，我还没有收到邮件。

Hi, David. I haven't got your e-mail.

A: Yěxǔ shì wǎngluò yǒu wèntí, wǒ zài fā gěi nǐ.
也许是网络有问题，我再发给你。

Maybe there is something wrong with the network. I'll send it to you again.

B: Wǒ de yóuxiāng shì zhèngcháng de, nǐ zài fā yí cì ba.
我的邮箱是正常的，你再发一次吧。

Shōudào yǐhòu wǒ gàosu nǐ.
收到以后我告诉你。

My mailbox is normal. Send it again. I'll let you know when I receive it.

New Words

1.	喂	wèi	叹 (interj.)	hello
2.	先生	xiānsheng	名 (n.)	Mr.
3.	位	wèi	量 (mw)	*measure word*
4.	通	tōng	动 (v.)	connect
5.	电话	diànhuà	名 (n.)	telephone
6.	哦	ò	叹 (interj.)	*used to indicate realization or understanding*

Lesson Eight I'm checking my mailbox on the internet.

7.	公司	gōngsī	名 (n.)	corporation, work
8.	工作	gōngzuò	名、动 (n./v.)	work; work
9.	开始	kāishǐ	动 (v.)	start
10.	给	gěi	动、介 (v./prep.)	give; for
11.	打	dǎ	动 (v.)	call
12.	告诉	gàosu	动 (v.)	tell
13.	手机	shǒujī	名 (n.)	mobile phone
14.	号码	hàomǎ	名 (n.)	number
15.	接	jiē	动 (v.)	answer
16.	出去	chū//qù	动 (v.)	be out
17.	记住	jìzhù	动 (v.)	remember
18.	麻烦	máfan	动、名 (v./n.)	trouble; trouble
19.	联系	liánxì	动 (v.)	contact
20.	收	shōu	动 (v.)	receive
21.	发	fā	动 (v.)	send
22.	电子邮件	diànzǐ yóujiàn		e-mail
	邮件	yóujiàn	名 (n.)	mail
23.	也许	yěxǔ	副 (adv.)	maybe
24.	网络	wǎngluò	名 (n.)	network
25.	邮箱	yóuxiāng	名 (n.)	mailbox
26.	正常	zhèngcháng	形 (adj.)	normal
27.	次	cì	量 (mw)	time

Chinese Crash Course

Proper Noun

刘涛   Liú Tāo   Liu Tao

Annotations

1. 喂   *wèi*

Chinese people use this word when they give sb. a call in order to get the person's attention, equivalent to hello in English.

2. 刘涛先生   *Liú Tāo xiānsheng*

To add "xiānsheng" or "xiǎojie" after a man or woman's name is a polite way to address people.

3. 位   *wèi*

The measure word "wèi" is a respectful form for modifying people. For example:

请问这位先生贵姓？

Excuse me, what's the gentleman's surname?

这位是李小姐。

This is Miss Li.

Lesson Eight I'm checking my mailbox on the internet.

4. 我给你打电话。 *Wǒ gěi nǐ dǎ diànhuà.*

The verb phrase "dǎ diànhuà" can't be followed by the object. We can't say "wǒ dǎ diànhuà nǐ". For example:

明天请给我打电话。

Please call me tomorrow.

昨天你给他打电话了吗?

Did you call him yesterday?

"Jiànmiàn" is used in the same way. We can say "wǒ hé tā jiànmiàn" but not "wǒ jiànmiàn tā".

5. 那我等你电话。 *Nà wǒ děng nǐ diànhuà.*

"Nà" here is a conjunction in spoken language. It leads to the due result of the previous sentence.

他不在家,那我晚上再打电话。

Since he isn't at home, I'll call again in the evening.

你今天没有时间,那明天呢?

You aren't free today. How about tomorrow?

那主食您要什么?

What would you like to have for principal food?

6. 号码的读法 *hàomǎ de dúfǎ*

We should read out every digit when a number is over three digits. And the same number should be repeated. For example:

四三零零一一五　　读作　　*sì sān líng líng yāo yāo wǔ*

four three zero zero one one five

7. 收到 *shōudào*

"Dào" in "shōudào", "kàndào" and "zhǎodào" serves as the complement of result of the verb before it. For example:

他来到了中国。

He has come to China.

我看到了老朋友。

I saw my old friend.

她找到了爱情。

She found her love.

8. 还没有收到 *hái méiyou shōudào*

"Hái" in this sentence indicates the condition remains unchanged. For example:

他还没有走。

He hasn't left yet.

他还在那个公司工作。

He still works in that company.

Exercises

一 完成句子 Complete the following sentences.

1. A：喂,你好,请问(　　　　)?
   B：他不在。

Lesson Eight *I'm checking my mailbox on the internet.*

2. A：请告诉我你的手机号码。

　　B：(　　　　　)。

3. A：现在我很忙，以后打电话吧。

　　B：好的，那我(　　　　　)。

二　选择　Choose the correct answers.

1. 他为什么不(　)我的电话？

　　A 想　　　B 给　　　C 接　　　D 找

2. 今天我没有时间，明天(　)给你打电话。

　　A 接　　　B 再　　　C 在　　　D 转

3. 请你(　　　　)，我晚上等你的电话。

　　A 电话　　B 电话我　　C 电话给我　　D 给我打电话

4. 请给我(　)电子邮件。

　　A 打　　　B 发　　　C 收　　　D 接

三　选词填空　Fill in the blanks with the proper words.

告诉　　位　　接　　开始　　工作　　再　　收到

1. 我是学生，我现在没有(　　　)。

2. 这个工作什么时候(　　　)？

3. 这(　　)先生姓李。

4. 没人(　　)电话，那我们明天(　　)打。

5. 请(　　)我您的电话号码。

6. 我还没有(　　)你的邮件。

Chinese Crash Course

Supplementary Words

1. 转	zhuǎn	动 (v.)	transfer
2. 总机	zǒngjī	名 (n.)	telephone exchange
3. 分机	fēnjī	名 (n.)	extension
4. 地址	dìzhǐ	名 (n.)	address
5. 清楚	qīngchu	形 (adj.)	clear
6. 接收	jiēshōu	动 (v.)	receive, accept
7. 查	chá	动 (v.)	check
8. 附件	fùjiàn	名 (n.)	appendix, accessory, attachment

Related Sentences

1. 请转1209房间。
   Qǐng zhuǎn yāo èr líng jiǔ fángjiān.
   Room 1209, please.
2. 这是分机。
   Zhè shì fēnjī.
   This is the extension.

Lesson Eight I'm checking my mailbox on the internet.

3. 邮件地址错了。

   Yóujiàn dìzhǐ cuò le.

   The address of the mail is wrong.

4. 电话听不清楚。

   Diànhuà tīng bu qīngchu.

   I can't hear you clearly on the phone.

5. 我给你发几张照片。

   Wǒ gěi nǐ fā jǐ zhāng zhàopiàn.

   I will send you some photos.

6. 喂,114,请帮我查一个电话号码。

   Wèi, yāo yāo sì, qǐng bāng wǒ chá yí ge diànhuà hàomǎ.

   Hello, please help me check a telephone number.

7. 我想找个网吧上网。

   Wǒ xiǎng zhǎo ge wǎngbā shàngwǎng.

   I want to find an internet cafe to surf the internet.

8. 保持联系。

   Bǎochí liánxì.

   Keep in touch.

9. 好久没有联系了,最近好吧?

   Hǎojiǔ méiyou liánxì le, zuìjìn hǎo ba?

   It has been a long time since we got in touch last time. How are you getting on?

10. 请看邮件的附件。

    Qǐng kàn yóujiàn de fùjiàn.

    Please read the attachment of the e-mail.

第 9 课 出租车!
Dì Jiǔ Kè Chūzūchē!
Lesson Nine Taxi!

Sentence Patterns

1. Wǒ xiǎng qù Yǒuyì Bīnguǎn.
   我想去友谊宾馆。
   I want to go to Youyi Hotel.

2. Wǒmen zǒu Yǒuyì Lù ba, nà tiáo lù chē shǎo.
   我们走友谊路吧,那条路车少。
   Let's take Youyi Road. There are fewer cars on that road.

3. Wǒ yǒu jí shì, nín néng bu néng kuài diǎnr?
   我有急事,您能不能快点儿?
   I have something urgent. Can you drive a little faster, please?

4. Nàr lí wǒmen zhèli tài yuǎn le.
   那儿离我们这里太远了。
   It's too far from here.

5. Wǒmen zuò gōnggòng qìchē háishi zuò dìtiě?
   我们坐公共汽车还是坐地铁?
   Do we take the bus or the subway?

6. Zǒu dào dìtiězhàn zhǐ yào wǔ fēnzhōng.
   走到地铁站只要五分钟。
   It only takes five minutes for us to walk to the subway station.

Lesson Nine Taxi!

**Dialogues**

      Chūzūchē!
A：出 租 车！

Hi, taxi!

      Nín hǎo, qǐngwèn nín xiǎng qù nǎr?
B：您好，请问您想去哪儿？

Hello, where do you want to go?

      Wǒ xiǎng qù Yǒuyì Bīnguǎn.
A：我想去友谊宾馆。

Yes, I'm going to Youyi Hotel.

Chinese Crash Course

Shàng chē ba.
B：上 车 吧。

Get on!

Shīfu, liù diǎn yǐqián néng dào Yǒuyì Bīnguǎn ma?
A：师 傅，6 点 以 前 能 到 友 谊 宾 馆 吗？

Sir, can we get there before six o'clock?

Bù yídìng, xiànzài chē duō.
B：不 一 定，现 在 车 多。

I'm not sure. There are too many cars on the road.

Wǒ yǒu jí shì, nín néng bu néng kuài diǎnr?
A：我 有 急 事，您 能 不 能 快 点 儿？

I have something urgent. Can you drive faster?

Wǒmen zǒu Yǒuyì Lù ba, nà tiáo lù chē shǎo.
B：我 们 走 友 谊 路 吧，那 条 路 车 少。

Let's take Youyi Road. There are fewer cars on that road.

Méi wèntí, liù diǎn dào jiù kěyǐ.
A：没 问 题，6 点 到 就 可 以。

It is all right if we get there at 6 o'clock.

Dàwèi, nǐ zhīdao Yǒuyì Bīnguǎn zěnme zǒu ma?
A：大 卫，你 知 道 友 谊 宾 馆 怎 么 走 吗？

David, do you know how to get to Youyi Hotel?

Lesson Nine Taxi!

B: Bù zhīdao. Wǒmen chá yíxià dìtú ba.
不知道。我们查一下地图吧。
Sorry, I don't know. Let's look up on the map.

A: Zhǎodào le! Nǐ kàn, lí wǒmen zhèli tài yuǎn le!
找到了！你看，离我们这里太远了！
I find it! You see, it's far away from here.

B: Zuò chūzūchē yǒu yìdiǎnr guì.
坐出租车有一点儿贵。
It's a little expensive to take the taxi.

A: Nà wǒmen zuò gōnggòng qìchē háishi zuò dìtiě?
那我们坐公共汽车还是坐地铁？
Do we take the bus or the subway?

B: Háishi zuò dìtiě ba. Gōnggòng qìchē tài màn le
还是坐地铁吧。公共汽车太慢了。
Let's take the subway. The bus is too slow.

Chinese Crash Course

A：Zuò dìtiě yě yào huàn chē.
坐 地 铁 也 要 换 车。

We also need to change lines when taking the subway.

B：Méi guānxi, huàn chē bù máfan.
没 关 系，换 车 不 麻 烦。

Never mind. It isn't troublesome to change lines.

A：Hǎo ba, xiànzài jiù chūfā ba!
好 吧，现 在 就 出 发 吧！

OK, let's go now!

B：Láidejí, zǒu dào dìtiězhàn zhǐ yào wǔ fēnzhōng.
来 得 及，走 到 地 铁 站 只 要 五 分 钟。

There is still time. It only takes five minutes to walk to the subway station.

New Words

1.	出租车	chūzūchē	名 (n.)	taxi
2.	友谊	yǒuyì	名 (n.)	friendship
3.	上车	shàng chē		get on the car
4.	师傅	shīfu	名 (n.)	master
5.	能	néng	助动 (auxil. v.)	can
6.	不一定	bù yídìng		not sure
7.	急事	jí shì		something urgent

Lesson Nine Taxi!

8.	路	lù	名 (n.)	road
9.	条	tiáo	量 (mw)	*measure word*
10.	少	shǎo	形 (adj.)	few
11.	地图	dìtú	名 (n.)	map
12.	离	lí	介、动 (prep./v.)	from; depart
13.	远	yuǎn	形 (adj.)	far
14.	坐	zuò	动 (v.)	take seat
15.	公共汽车	gōnggòng qìchē		bus
16.	还是	háishi	连、副 (conj./adv.)	still
17.	地铁	dìtiě	名 (n.)	subway
18.	慢	màn	形 (adj.)	slow
19.	要	yào	助动 (auxil. v.)	need
20.	换	huàn	动 (v.)	change
21.	出发	chūfā	动 (v.)	start
22.	地铁站	dìtiězhàn	名 (n.)	subway station
23.	只	zhǐ	副 (adv.)	only

Annotations

1. 能 *néng*

The optative verb "néng" indicates the ability could be reached or being qualified for something. It also indicates possibility. The negative

form is "bù néng" or "méi néng". For example:

你能告诉他吗?

Can you tell him?

他能来晚会吗?

Can he come to the evening party?

今天我们能见面吗?

Can we meet today?

明天我不能等你了。

I can't wait for you tomorrow.

2. 离我们这里太远了　　　*lí wǒmen zhèli tài yuǎn le*

"A lí B" is a commonly used form to indicate distance and location in Chinese. For example:

网吧离书店很远。

The internet cafe is far from the bookshop.

中国离韩国很近,离美国很远。

China is near to South Korea, but is far from America.

3. 坐公共汽车还是坐地铁?　　　*Zuò gōnggòng qìchē háishi zuò dìtiě?*

"A háishi B?" is an alternative question. When answering it, you can't use "duì" or "bú shì". For example:

你去书店还是网吧?　　　——　　　我去网吧。

Do you want to go to the bookshop or the internet cafe? —— I want to go to the internet cafe.

Lesson Nine   Taxi!

你喜欢她还是那个女孩？　　——　　当然是那个女孩！
Do you like her or that girl?　——　Of course I like that girl!
你的生日是明天还是后天？　——　后天。
Is your birthday tomorrow or the day after tomorrow? ——
It is the day after tomorrow.

4. 要　yào

"Yào" indicates that someone hopes to get something or need or have to do something. For example:

坐地铁要换三次车。

You have to change the lines for three times when taking the subway.

从这里到车站要走十分钟。

It takes ten minutes to walk from here to the station.

5. 就　jiù

The adverb "jiù" indicates that something happens in a very short time. For example:

他很快就到了。

He will arrive soon.

现在就出发吧。

Let's start now.

6. 只　zhǐ

"Zhǐ" is an adverb which limits the scope. For example:

我只点了一个菜，别的你点吧。

I only ordered one dish. You order something else, please.

Chinese Crash Course

那本书的价格只有两块钱。

The price of that book is only two yuan.

一 完成句子 Complete the following sentences.

1. 出租车师傅：您现在去哪儿？

 大　　卫：（　　　　　）。

2. A：你能找到他吗？

 B：（　　　　　）。

3. A：我们现在去网吧还是去卡拉OK (karaoke)？

 B：当然（　　　　　）。

二 选择 Choose the correct answers.

1. 你的房间（　）图书馆远吗？

 A 和　　　　B 是　　　　C 找　　　　D 离

2. 我们不（　）去那个地方，路太远了！

 A 可以　　　B 能　　　　C 换　　　　D 走

3. 我们坐地铁到那里，再（　　）公共汽车。

 A 要　　　　B 看　　　　C 换　　　　D 麻烦

4. 坐出租车很快，但是（　　　）贵。

 A 一点儿　　B 点儿有　　C 有点儿　　D 有很

Lesson Nine Taxi!

三、选词填空 Fill in the blanks with the proper words.

离　换　麻烦　能　还是　就

1. 坐公共汽车太(　　)了,要换车。
2. 明天我想(　　)到1209房间,我不喜欢1208房间。
3. 你(　　)来我们的晚会吗?
4. 他是艾玛的哥哥(　　)朋友?
5. 那个宾馆(　　)这儿很远吗?
6. 我打电话了,出租车很快(　　)到了。

Supplementary Words

1. 公共汽车站	gōnggòng qìchēzhàn		bus stop
2. 打车	dǎ//chē	动 (v.)	take a taxi
3. 发票	fāpiào	名 (n.)	invoice
4. 里程表	lǐchéngbiǎo	名 (n.)	odometer
5. 环城铁路	huánchéng tiělù		railway round the city
6. 下一站	xià yí zhàn		next stop
7. 堵车(塞车)	dǔ//chē(sāi//chē)		traffic jam
8. 高峰时间	gāofēng shíjiān		rush hour
9. 交通	jiāotōng	名 (n.)	traffic

Chinese Crash Course

Related Sentences

1. 从这儿到那儿大概要多长时间?

    Cóng zhèr dào nàr dàgài yào duō cháng shíjiān?

    How long will it take to get from here to that place?

2. 换个路线吧。

    Huàn ge lùxiàn ba.

    Let's change the route.

3. 要坐六站才到。

    Yào zuò liù zhàn cái dào.

    It takes 6 stops to get there.

4. 问售票员到哪里下车。

    Wèn shòupiàoyuán dào nǎli xià chē.

    You can ask the conductor that where you should get off.

5. 这条路常常堵车。

    Zhè tiáo lù chángcháng dǔchē.

    This road is often congested with traffic.

6. 现在是高峰时间。

    Xiànzài shì gāofēng shíjiān.

    Now is the rush hour.

7. 走这条路可能会绕一点儿路。

    Zǒu zhè tiáo lù kěnéng huì rào yìdiǎnr lù.

    If we take this road, we might take a longer route.

Lesson Nine Taxi!

8. 车费一共是23元。

   Chēfèi yígòng shì èrshísān yuán.

   The fare is 23 yuan totally.

第 10 课　这件上衣我最满意！
Lesson Ten　This is the coat that I am most satisfied with!

Sentence Patterns

1. Jīntiān wǒ yào qù mǎi jǐ jiàn yīfu.
   今天我要去买几件衣服。
   I'm going to buy some clothes today.

2. Nǐ chuān qípáo yídìng fēicháng piàoliang.
   你穿旗袍一定非常漂亮。
   You must look very beautiful when you are in cheongsam.

3. Yǒuyì Lù yǒu yì jiā shāngchǎng.
   友谊路有一家商场。
   There is a shop on the Youyi Road.

4. Shāngchǎng gānggāng kāiyè, dōngxi yídìng yòu piányi yòu hǎo.
   商场刚刚开业，东西一定又便宜又好。
   The shop is just open. Things there must be cheap and good.

5. Huānyíng liǎng wèi lái wǒmen shāngchǎng!
   欢迎两位来我们商场！
   Welcome to our shop!

Lesson Ten This is the coat that I am most satisfied with!

    Wǒ shì yíxià zhè jiàn shàngyī, kěyǐ ma?
6. 我 试 一 下 这 件 上 衣，可 以 吗?
   May I try on this coat, please?

    Jiàgé hé yàngshì wǒ dōu mǎnyì.
7. 价 格 和 样 式 我 都 满 意。
   I'm satisfied with the price and the style.

    Wǒ mǎidàole zuì mǎnyì de dōngxi.
8. 我 买 到 了 最 满 意 的 东 西。
   I bought the thing that I am most satisfied with.

    Zhè jiàn cái bāshí yuán.
9. 这 件 才 八 十 元。
   This one is only 80 yuan.

    Jīntiān wǒ yào qù mǎi jǐ jiàn yīfu.
A: 今 天 我 要 去 买 几 件 衣 服。

   I'm going to buy some clothes today.

    Wǒ yě xiǎng mǎi yí jiàn qípáo, wǎnhuì de shíhou chuān.
B: 我 也 想 买 一 件 旗 袍，晚 会 的 时 候 穿。

   I also want to buy a cheongsam and wear it when I attend the evening party.

Chinese Crash Course

A: Nǐ chuān qípáo yídìng fēicháng piàoliang!
你 穿 旗 袍 一 定 非 常 漂 亮！

You must look very beautiful when you are in cheongsam!

B: Wǒmen qù nǎ jiā shāngchǎng ne?
我 们 去 哪 家 商 场 呢？

Which shop shall we go to?

A: Yǒuyì Lù yǒu yì jiā shāngchǎng, gānggāng kāiyè.
友 谊 路 有 一 家 商 场， 刚 刚 开 业。

There is a shop on Youyi Road and it is just open.

B: Dōngxi yídìng yòu piányi yòu hǎo.
东 西 一 定 又 便 宜 又 好。

Things there must be cheap and good.

A: Wǒ hái xiǎng mǎi yìdiǎnr xiǎo lǐpǐn.
我 还 想 买 一 点 儿 小 礼 品。

I also want to buy some small gifts.

Lesson Ten This is the coat that I am most satisfied with!

B: Zǒu ba, wǒ zài mǎi diǎnr huàzhuāngpǐn.
走吧，我再买点儿化妆品。

Let's go. I also want to buy some cosmetics.

C: Huānyíng liǎng wèi xiǎojie lái wǒmen shāngchǎng, nǐmen xiǎng mǎi shénme?
欢迎两位小姐来我们商场，你们想买什么？

Welcome you two ladies to our shop. What would you like to buy?

A: Qǐngwèn, mǎi fúzhuāng zài jǐ céng?
请问，买服装在几层？

Excuse me, on which floor can we buy clothes?

C: Nán shì fúzhuāng zài èr lóu, nǚ shì fúzhuāng zài sān lóu.
男式服装在二楼，女式服装在三楼。

Male dress is on the second floor, and female dress is on the third floor.

(bàn ge xiǎoshí yǐhòu)
(半个小时以后)

(half an hour later)

B: Wǒ shìle jǐ jiàn qípáo.
我试了几件旗袍。

I tried on a few cheongsams.

Chinese Crash Course

Jiàgé hé yàngshì dōu héshì ma?
A：价格和样式都合适吗？

Are the price and the style OK for you?

Jiàgé hái kěyǐ, kěshì yàngshì bú shìhé wǒ.
B：价格还可以，可是样式不适合我。

The price is just OK, but the style doesn't suit me.

Xiǎo lǐpǐn hěn duō, dànshì yòu piányi yòu hǎo de tài shǎo le.
A：小礼品很多，但是又便宜又好的太少了。

There are a lot of small gifts. But there are few cheap and good ones.

Nǐ méi mǎidào dōngxi ma?
B：你没买到东西吗？

Didn't you buy anything?

Lesson Ten This is the coat that I am most satisfied with!

A：
Mǎidàole, zhè jiàn shàngyī wǒ zuì mǎnyì!
买 到 了，这 件 上 衣 我 最 满 意！

Yes. I'm most satisfied with the coat.

B：
Duōshao qián?
多 少 钱？

How much is it?

A：
Cái bāshí yuán.
才 八 十 元。

It's only 80 yuan.

New Words

1.	买	mǎi	动 (v.)	buy
2.	件	jiàn	量 (mw)	piece
3.	衣服	yīfu	名 (n.)	clothes
4.	旗袍	qípáo	名 (n.)	cheongsam
5.	穿	chuān	动 (v.)	put on
6.	非常	fēicháng	副 (adv.)	very
7.	商场	shāngchǎng	名 (n.)	shop
8.	刚刚	gānggāng	副 (adv.)	just
9.	开业	kāi//yè	动 (v.)	open
10.	又	yòu	副 (adv.)	as well

Chinese Crash Course

11.	便宜	piányi	形 (adj.)	cheap
12.	礼品	lǐpǐn	名 (n.)	present, gift
13.	化妆品	huàzhuāngpǐn	名 (n.)	cosmetic
14.	服装	fúzhuāng	名 (n.)	dress
15.	楼	lóu	名 (n.)	floor
16.	男式	nán shì		male style
	式	shì	名 (n.)	style
17.	女式	nǚ shì		female style
18.	试	shì	动 (v.)	try on
19.	价格	jiàgé	名 (n.)	price
20.	样式	yàngshì	名 (n.)	style
21.	合适	héshì	形 (adj.)	fit; suit
22.	上衣	shàngyī	名 (n.)	coat
23.	最	zuì	副 (adv.)	most
24.	满意	mǎnyì	形 (adj.)	satisfied
25.	多少钱	duōshao qián		how much
26.	才	cái	副 (adv.)	only
27.	元	yuán	名 (n.)	yuan

Lesson Ten This is the coat that I am most satisfied with!

Annotations

1. **晚会的时候穿/晚会时穿**

   wǎnhuì de shíhou chuān / wǎnhuì shí chuān

   "……de shíhou" or "……shí" is a time adverbial. You can't say "……shíhou" or "……de shí". For example:

   我上课的时候看到了王老师。

   I saw Teacher Wang when I attended the class.

   商场开业时人非常多。

   There were many people when the shop was just opened to the public.

   我生日的时候朋友给了我很多东西。

   My friends gave me many presents on my birthday.

2. **我们去哪家商场呢?**   *Wǒmen qù nǎ jiā shāngchǎng ne?*

   The interrogative pronoun "nǎ" can not directly modify a noun. It needs to be followed by a measure word which indicates the sort and the characteristic of the noun. For example:

   A: 哪位老师是你的汉语老师?

   Which teacher is your Chinese teacher?

   B: 那位女老师是。

   That woman teacher.

   A: 哪个是你的词典?

   Which one is your dictionary?

B：小的那个。

That little one.

3. 刚刚　　gānggāng

"Gānggāng" or "gāng" is an adverb, indicating the action or the situation just happened. For example:

他刚走。

He left just now.

我刚刚起床,不知道现在几点。

I just got up and didn't know what time it is now.

他刚来这里工作。

He came to work here not long ago.

4. 又便宜又好　　yòu piányi yòu hǎo

The coordinate use of "yòu" indicates the coexistence of several situations or attributes. For example:

今天的菜又好吃又好看。

The dish of today is both delicious and good-looking.

坐地铁又快又便宜。

It is cheap and fast to take the subway.

5. 我最满意。　　Wǒ zuì mǎnyì.

The adverb "zuì" is put before an adjective. It indicates the superlative degree which nothing will excel. For example:

Lesson Ten This is the coat that I am most satisfied with!

那个女孩最漂亮。

That girl is the most beautiful one.

这个菜最好吃。

This dish is the most delicious one.

这个商场的东西最便宜。

Things in this shop are the cheapest.

7. 多少　duōshao

The interrogative pronoun "duōshao" is used for enquiring quantity or number. For example:

昨天来了多少人？

How many people came yesterday?

我们还有多少时间？

How much time do we have?

6. 才　cái

The adverb "cái" can indicate the time is short or early; the number is small or the degree is low.

才六点，太早了。

It is too early. It is just six o'clock.

四个人吃饭，他才点了两个菜。

He only ordered two dishes when they four had meals.

他才20岁，太年轻了。

He is only twenty years old. He is too young.

Chinese Crash Course

一 完成句子　Complete the following sentences.

1. 售货员：欢迎您，请问您买什么？
   艾　玛：(　　　　　　)。
   售货员：您试一试这件上衣。满意吗？
   艾　玛：(　　　　　　)。
2. 艾玛：这件旗袍怎么样？
   铃木：(　　　　　　)。

二 选择　Choose the correct answers.

1. 这件衣服样式很好，但是价格有点儿(　　)。
   　A 便宜　　B 多　　C 大　　D 贵
2. 你穿这(　)旗袍一定非常漂亮。
   　A 些　　B 个　　C 件　　D 一
3. 他(　)来这里工作，我不认识他。
   　A 又　　B 刚　　C 多　　D 就
4. 昨天这家商场(　　)，有很多人来买东西。
   　A 欢迎　　B 买到　　C 开始　　D 开业
5. 这个电子词典是(　　)好的。
   　A 刚刚　　B 刚　　C 多　　D 最

Lesson Ten This is the coat that I am most satisfied with!

 三　选词填空　Fill in the blanks with the proper words.

多少　　满意　　最　　刚刚　　又……又……　　样式

1. 那件上衣的（　　）最漂亮！
2. 这个菜（　　）辣（　　）油腻。
3. 我（　　）起床，电话就来了。
4. 这件上衣价格是（　　）？
5. 青岛啤酒（　　）好。
6. 这件旗袍的样式您（　　）吗？

Supplementary Words

1.	价钱	jiàqián	名 (n.)	price
2.	款式	kuǎnshì	名 (n.)	style
3.	商品	shāngpǐn	名 (n.)	commodity
4.	百货	bǎihuò	名 (n.)	general merchandise
5.	生活用品	shēnghuó yòngpǐn		daily necessities
6.	购物	gòu wù		go shopping
7.	逛	guàng	动 (v.)	stroll
8.	打折	dǎ//zhé	动 (v.)	discount
9.	优惠	yōuhuì	动、形 (v./adj.)	favor; favorable
10.	电器	diànqì	名 (n.)	electric appliances
11.	家电	jiādiàn	名 (n.)	household electronic applicances

12. 现金	xiànjīn	名(n.)	cash
13. 刷卡	shuā//kǎ	动(v.)	pay with the credit card
14. 售货员	shòuhuòyuán	名(n.)	salesperson

Related Sentences

1. 她是个购物狂。
   Tā shì ge gòuwùkuáng.
   She's crazy about shopping.

2. 这是最新款的商品。
   Zhè shì zuì xīn kuǎn de shāngpǐn.
   This is the commodity of the latest style.

3. 这件衣服打折了。
   Zhè jiàn yīfu dǎzhé le.
   This garment is on sale.

4. 我想买电器。
   Wǒ xiǎng mǎi diànqì.
   I would like to buy electric appliance.

5. 请问家电在几层?
   Qǐngwèn jiādiàn zài jǐ céng?
   Excuse me, which floor sells household electric appliances?

6. 您刷卡还是用现金?
   Nín shuākǎ háishi yòng xiànjīn?
   Would you like to pay with the credit card or cash?

第 11 课 我参加了一个中文辅导班。
Dì Shíyī Kè Wǒ cānjiāle yí ge Zhōngwén fǔdǎobān.

Lesson Eleven   I attend a Chinese tutoring class.

Sentence Patterns

1. 您是咨询还是报名？
   Nín shì zīxún háishi bàomíng?
   Would you like to consult or register?

2. 我报中级班。
   Wǒ bào zhōngjí bān.
   I want to sign up for the intermediate class.

3. 先交学费，然后再领教材。
   Xiān jiāo xuéfèi, ránhòu zài lǐng jiàocái.
   You should pay your tuition first, and then go to get your teaching materials.

4. 你会说汉语吗？
   Nǐ huì shuō Hànyǔ ma?
   Can you speak Chinese?

5. Wǒ huì yìdiǎnr Hànyǔ.
   我 会 一 点 儿 汉 语。

   I can speak a little Chinese.

6. Wǒmen gōngsī xūyào yí wèi fānyì.
   我 们 公 司 需 要 一 位 翻 译。

   Our company needs an interpreter.

7. Nǐ kěyǐ yìbiān gōngzuò yìbiān xuéxí.
   你 可 以 一 边 工 作 一 边 学 习。

   You can work and at the same time study.

8. Nǐ de Hànyǔ jìnbù hěn kuài.
   你 的 汉 语 进 步 很 快。

   You have made rapid progress in your Chinese.

9. Yǐqián wǒ méiyou xuéguo Hànyǔ.
   以 前 我 没 有 学 过 汉 语。

   I haven't learned Chinese before.

10. Wǒ cānjiāle yí ge Zhōngwén fǔdǎobān.
    我 参 加 了 一 个 中 文 辅 导 班。

    I take part in a Chinese tutoring class.

11. Nǐ shì shénme shíhou kāishǐ xuéxí Hànyǔ de?
    你 是 什 么 时 候 开 始 学 习 汉 语 的?

    When did you begin to learn Chinese?

12. Zhè shì ge hǎo jīhuì.
    这 是 个 好 机 会。

    This is a good chance.

Lesson Eleven I attend a Chinese tutoring class.

Dialogues

Nǐ hǎo, zhèli shì Zhōngwén fǔdǎobān ma?
A：你好，这里是中文辅导班吗？

Hello, is this the Chinese tutoring class?

Duì, nín shì zīxún háishi bàomíng?
B：对，您是咨询还是报名？

Yes, do you consult or sign up for a class?

Wǒ kànguo nǐmen de guǎnggào le, wǒ shì lái bàomíng de.
A：我看过你们的广告了，我是来报名的。

Chinese Crash Course

I have read your advertisement. I come to sign up for it.

B: Hǎo, nín zhǔnbèi cānjiā nǎge bān?
好，您准备参加哪个班？

OK. Which class do you want to take?

A: Wǒ bào zhōngjí bān.
我报中级班。

I want to take the intermediate class.

B: Nín xiān qù nàbiān jiāo xuéfèi, ránhòu lǐng jiàocái.
您先去那边交学费，然后领教材。

You can pay your tuition first, and then get your teaching materials.

A: Xièxie!
谢谢！

Thank you!

A: Dàwèi, nǐ huì shuō Hànyǔ ma?
大卫，你会说汉语吗？

David, can you speak Chinese?

B: Huì yìdiǎnr.
会一点儿。

I speak a little Chinese.

A: Wǒmen gōngsī xūyào yí wèi fānyì.
我们公司需要一位翻译。

Our company needs an interpreter.

Lesson Eleven I attend a Chinese tutoring class.

B: Wǒ de shuǐpíng kěnéng bù xíng.
我的水平可能不行。

Sorry, I'm afraid I can't.

A: Nǐ kěyǐ yìbiān gōngzuò yìbiān xuéxí.
你可以一边工作一边学习。

You can work and at the same time study.

B: Wǒ cānjiāle yí ge Zhōngwén fǔdǎobān, jìnbù hěn kuài.
我参加了一个中文辅导班,进步很快。

I have taken part in a Chinese tutoring class and made fast progress.

A: Hǎo jí le! Sān ge yuè yǐhòu, nǐ yídìng huì yǒu hěn dà de jìnbù.
好极了!三个月以后,你一定会有很大的进步。

That's great! Your Chinese will be improved a lot after three months.

A: Qǐngwèn, dào Zhōngguó yǐqián, nǐ xuéxíguo Hànyǔ ma?
请问,到中国以前,你学习过汉语吗?

Excuse me, have you learned Chinese before you came to China?

B: Méiyou xuéguo.
没有学过。

No, I haven't.

A: Nǐ shì shénme shíhou kāishǐ xuéxí Hànyǔ de?
你是什么时候开始学习汉语的?

When did you begin to learn Chinese?

B: Lái Zhōngguó yǐhòu.
来中国以后。

After I came to China.

A: Shì zài shénme dìfang xué de?
是在什么地方学的?

Where did you study Chinese?

B: Báitiān zài wàiyǔ dàxué xuéxí, wǎnshang cānjiā fǔdǎobān.
白天在外语大学学习,晚上参加辅导班。

I studied at the Foreign Languages University in the daytime, and take a tutoring class at night.

Lesson Eleven I attend a Chinese tutoring class.

A: Cānjiāguo Hànyǔ Shuǐpíng Kǎoshì ma?
参加过汉语水平考试吗？

Did you take the HSK?

B: Kǎoguo HSK, qùnián bā yuè shí wǒ de chéngjì shì qī jí.
考过 HSK，去年 8 月时我的成绩是 7 级。

Yes, I passed HSK (7 level) last August.

A: Hǎo jí le! Nǐ xǐhuan dào wǒmen gōngsī gōngzuò ma?
好极了！你喜欢到我们公司工作吗？

That's great! Would you like to work at our company?

B: Dāngrán, zhè shì ge hǎo jīhui.
当然，这是个好机会。

Certainly, it's a great opportunity for me.

New Words

1.	中文	Zhōngwén	名 (n.)	Chinese
2.	辅导班	fǔdǎobān	名 (n.)	tutoring class
	辅导	fǔdǎo	动 (v.)	tutor
3.	咨询	zīxún	动 (v.)	consult
4.	报名	bào//míng	动 (v.)	sign up
5.	广告	guǎnggào	名 (n.)	advertisement
6.	参加	cānjiā	动 (v.)	take part in
7.	中级	zhōngjí	名 (n.)	intermediate level
8.	交	jiāo	动 (v.)	hand in, pay
9.	学费	xuéfèi	名 (n.)	tuition
10.	然后	ránhòu	连 (conj.)	then
11.	领	lǐng	动 (v.)	take
12.	教材	jiàocái	名 (n.)	teaching material
13.	说	shuō	动 (v.)	speak
14.	翻译	fānyì	动、名 (v./n.)	translate; interpreter
15.	水平	shuǐpíng	名 (n.)	level
16.	可能	kěnéng	副 (adv.)	maybe
17.	行	xíng	形 (adj.)	possible
18.	一边……一边……	yìbiān……yìbiān……		at the same time
19.	学习	xuéxí	动 (v.)	study, learn

Lesson Eleven I attend a Chinese tutoring class.

20.	进步	jìnbù	动 (v.)	make progress
21.	极	jí	副 (adv.)	very
22.	白天	báitiān	名 (n.)	daytime
23.	外语	wàiyǔ	名 (n.)	foreign language
24.	大学	dàxué	名 (n.)	university
25.	考试	kǎoshì	动、名 (v./n.)	test; test
26.	去年	qùnián	名 (n.)	last year
27.	成绩	chéngjì	名 (n.)	score
28.	机会	jīhuì	名 (n.)	chance, opportunity

Proper Noun

HSK 考试   HSK kǎoshì
(汉语水平考试)   (Hànyǔ Shuǐpíng Kǎoshì)   HSK test

Annotations

1. 可能不行   *kěnéng bù xíng*

"Xíng" means agreement or permission. In most cases, it is used in an answer. For example:

你可以来我们公司吗? ——行,我下午去。
Can you come to our company?——OK, I'll be there in the afternoon.
我有这个机会吗? ——不行,你不会汉语。
Can I have the chance? ——Sorry, you don't know Chinese.

2. 一边工作一边学习　　yìbiān gōngzuò yìbiān xuéxí

"Yìbiān…… yìbiān……" indicates the subject does two things at the same time. "Yì" can be omitted. For example:

我们一边走一边说。
We talk while walking together.
他边喝酒边吃饭。
He drinks while eating.

3. 好极了　　hǎo jí le

The adverb "jí" indicates that it has reached the top degree. It functions as a complement after an adjective.

我最近忙极了!
I'm very busy in these days!
她穿旗袍漂亮极了!
She's so beautiful wearing this cheongsam.

4. 没有学过汉语　　méiyou xuéguo Hànyǔ

"Guo" here acts as a verb termination indicating the completion of an action. It also indicates some action or change has happened before. This kind of action is influential to the present. "Méi / méiyou" is used to

Lesson Eleven　I attend a Chinese tutoring class.

form the negation. For example:

你们吃过饭再走吧！

Please have dinner here before you leave!

他来过上海。

He has been to Shanghai.

我看过你们的广告了。

I have seen your advertisement.

我没看过他的女朋友。

I haven't seen his girlfriend.

5. 是什么时候学的？/ 是在什么地方学的？

Shì shénme shíhou xué de? / Shì zài shénme dìfang xué de?

The structure "shì …… de" emphasizes the time, place, agent or manner of a past action. For example:

你是什么时候来的中国？　　——去年２月。
When did you come to China?　——Last February.

你是在哪里买的旗袍？　　　——友谊商场。
Where did you buy the cheongsam?　——At Youyi Store.

是谁告诉你的？　　　　　　——我的同学。
Who told you?　　　　　　——My classmate.

你是怎么来的？　　　　　　——坐出租汽车。
How did you come here?　　——By a taxi.

Chinese Crash Course

Exercises

一　完成句子　Complete the following sentences.

1. A：你会中文吗？
   B：（　　　　　）。

2. A：你的汉语有进步吗？
   B：（　　　　　）。

3. A：您是什么时候开始学的汉语？
   B：（　　　　　）。

二　选择　Choose the correct answers.

1. 我是去年来（　）中国。
   A 到　　　B 了　　　C 的　　　D 在

2. 我（　）在辅导班学的汉语。
   A 不　　　B 没　　　C 不是　　D 还

3. 他的汉语好（　　）了！
   A 大　　　B 太　　　C 极　　　D 非常

4. 我在澳大利亚工作（　），现在在中国学习汉语。
   A 没　　　B 的　　　C 过　　　D 有

5. 他们（　）走边看。
   A 一边　　B 边　　　C 又　　　D 是

Lesson Eleven I attend a Chinese tutoring class.

三 选词填空 Fill in the blanks with proper words.

进步　成绩　过　机会　可能

1. 明天他(　　)不能来上课了。
2. 我没吃(　　)烤鸭。
3. 你的汉语(　　)非常大。
4. 他的考试(　　)不怎么样。
5. 这是个好(　　)，你一定要去。

Supplementary Words

1. 交费	jiāo fèi		pay the fee
2. 学时	xuéshí	名 (n.)	class period
3. 任课教师	rènkè jiàoshī		instructor
4. 课程	kèchéng	名 (n.)	course
5. 安排	ānpái	动、名 (v./n.)	arrange; arrangement
6. 登记	dēngjì	动 (v.)	check in
7. 手续	shǒuxù	名 (n.)	procedure
8. 入学	rù//xué	动 (v.)	enroll
9. 开学	kāi//xué	动 (v.)	term begins

Chinese Crash Course

Related Sentences

1. 什么时候开学？
   Shénme shíhou kāixué?
   When does the school begin?

2. 谁是任课教师？
   Shuí shì rènkè jiàoshī?
   Who's the instructor?

3. 每周几课时？
   Měi zhōu jǐ kèshí?
   How many classes are there every week?

4. 你的汉语程度怎么样？
   Nǐ de Hànyǔ chéngdù zěnmeyàng?
   What's your Chinese level?

5. 我去HSK辅导班报名。
   Wǒ qù HSK fǔdǎobān bàomíng.
   I'm going to sign up for the HSK tutoring class.

第 12 课 您用航空邮寄还是普通邮寄？

Dì Shí'èr Kè Nín yòng hángkōng yóujì háishi pǔtōng yóujì?

Lesson Twelve Do you want to post it by air mail or ordinary mail?

Sentence Patterns

1. 从澳大利亚寄来的邮件到了。
   Cóng Àodàlìyà jìlái de yóujiàn dào le.
   The mail from Australia has arrived.

2. 我妈妈寄给我的。
   Wǒ māma jìgěi wǒ de.
   It is my mother who sent me this.

3. 到哪里去取邮件呢？
   Dào nǎli qù qǔ yóujiàn ne?
   Where can I get the mail?

4. 我给上海的朋友寄一本书。
   Wǒ gěi Shànghǎi de péngyou jì yì běn shū.
   I'm sending a book to my friend in Shanghai.

5. 你可以办理快递业务。
   Nǐ kěyǐ bànlǐ kuàidì yèwù.
   You can use the EMS.

Chinese Crash Course

Yòng hángkōng yóujì háishi pǔtōng yóujì?
6. 用航空邮寄还是普通邮寄？

Do you want to post the it by air nail or ordinary mail?

Qǐng tián yíxià zhè zhāng biǎo.
7. 请填一下这张表。

Fill in this form, please.

Dialogues

Àimǎ, nǐ de yóujiàn dào le, shì cóng Àodàlìyà jì-
A: 艾玛，你的邮件到了，是从澳大利亚寄
lái de.
来的。

Emma, your mail has arrived. It is from Australia.

Yídìng shì wǒ māma jìgěi wǒ de. Dào nǎli qù
B: 一定是我妈妈寄给我的。到哪里去
qǔ ne?
取呢？

It must be my mother who sent it to me. Where can I get it?

Lesson Twelve   Do you want to post it by air mail or ordinary mail?

A: Yóujiàn tōngzhīdān shang xiě zhene, jiù zài fùjìn nàge yóujú.
邮件 通知单 上 写 着 呢，就 在 附近 那个 邮局。

It is written on the postal notification. It is the post office nearby.

B: Wǒ yào dài shénme zhèngjiàn ne?
我 要 带 什么 证件 呢?

What certificate do I need to take?

A: Dài shēnfènzhèng jiù kěyǐ lǐngqǔ le.
带 身份证 就 可以 领取 了。

You can get it with your ID card.

Chinese Crash Course

A：Nǐ qù yóujú jì shénme?
你 去 邮 局 寄 什 么？

What are you going to post at the post office?

B：Wǒ gěi Shànghǎi de péngyou jì yì běn shū, tā fēicháng zháojí.
我 给 上 海 的 朋 友 寄 一 本 书，他 非 常 着 急。

I'm going to send a book to a friend in Shanghai. He is anxious to have it.

A：Nǐ kěyǐ bànlǐ kuàidì yèwù, "tè kuài zhuān dì" zuì kuài.
你 可 以 办 理 快 递 业 务，"特 快 专 递"最 快。

You can use the express delivery. The EMS is the fastest.

Lesson Twelve Do you want to post it by air mail or ordinary mail?

B：Dàgài duōshao qián?
大概多少钱?

How much is it?

A：Bù yídìng, jǐ shí kuài dào jǐ bǎi kuài.
不一定,几十块到几百块。

I'm not sure, from several dozen yuan to several hundred yuan.

A：Nǐ hǎo, wǒ yào jì jǐ běn shū, qǐngwèn zěnme bànlǐ?
你好,我要寄几本书,请问怎么办理?

Hello. I want to send some books. What formalities should I go through?

B：Jìdào nǎlǐ?
寄到哪里?

Where do you want to send it?

A: Jìdào Rìběn.
寄 到 日 本。

To Japan.

B: Nín yòng hángkōng yóujì háishi pǔtōng yóujì?
您 用 航 空 邮 寄 还 是 普 通 邮 寄？

Do you want to post them by air mail or ordinary mail?

A: Nàbiān bù zháojí, wǒ yòng pǔtōng yóujì jiù kěyǐ.
那 边 不 着 急, 我 用 普 通 邮 寄 就 可 以。

It's not urgent. I can send them by ordinary mail.

B: Qǐng tián yíxià zhè zhāng biǎo, wǒ gěi nín chēng yíxià zhòngliàng.
请 填 一 下 这 张 表, 我 给 您 称 一 下 重 量。

Fill in this form, please. I will weigh them for you.

A: Duōshao qián?
多 少 钱？

How much is it?

B: Yìbǎi líng wǔ kuài.
一 百 零 五 块。

One hundred and five yuan.

New Words

1. 从   cóng   介 (prep.)   from

Lesson Twelve Do you want to post it by air mail or ordinary mail?

2. 取	qǔ	动 (v.)		take
3. 通知单	tōngzhīdān	名 (n.)		notification
通知	tōngzhī	动、名 (v./n.)		give notice; notice
4. 写	xiě	动 (v.)		write
5. 着呢	zhene	助 (part.)		*used to indicate a state*
6. 带	dài	动 (v.)		take
7. 证件	zhèngjiàn	名 (n.)		certificate
8. 身份证	shēnfènzhèng	名 (n.)		ID card
9. 领取	lǐngqǔ	动 (v.)		draw, get
10. 着急	zháo//jí	形 (adj.)		anxious, worried
11. 办理	bànlǐ	动 (v.)		do
12. 快递	kuàidì	名 (n.)		express delivery
13. 业务	yèwù	名 (n.)		business
14. 大概	dàgài	副 (adv.)		probably
15. 块	kuài	量 (mw)		yuan
16. 百	bǎi	数 (num.)		hundred
17. 航空	hángkōng	名 (n.)		air
18. 邮寄	yóujì	动 (v.)		post
19. 普通	pǔtōng	形 (adj.)		ordinary
20. 填	tián	动 (v.)		fill in
21. 张	zhāng	量 (mw)		piece

Chinese Crash Course

22.	表	biǎo	名 (n.)	table, form
23.	称	chēng	动 (v.)	weigh
24.	重量	zhòngliàng	名 (n.)	weight
25.	零	líng	数 (num.)	zero

Proper Noun

特快专递(EMS)　　tè kuài zhuān dì (EMS)　　　　　EMS

Annotations

1. 从澳大利亚寄来　　cóng Àodàlìyà jìlái

Prepositions "cóng", "lí", "gěi" can form prepositional phrase with the object, serving as the adverbial. For example:

他们从商场里出来了。

They come out from the shop.

我们从中国来。

We come from China.

我们从这儿走吧。

Let's go this way.

Lesson Twelve   Do you want to post it by air mail or ordinary mail?

2. 到哪里去取呢？/带什么呢？   Dào nǎli qù qǔ ne? / Dài shénme ne?

"Ne" is used at the end of a sentence to express enquiry. For example:

你说什么呢？

What are you talking about?

他来呢？还是不来呢？

Does he come or not?

她为什么不接电话呢？

Why didn't she answer the phone?

3. 怎么办理   zěnme bànlǐ

The interrogative pronoun "zěnme" can be used to ask property, manner, situation and reason. For example:

你是怎么来的？ ——坐地铁。

How did you come? ——By subway.

见面以后你怎么说？ ——我都告诉他。

What will you say when you meet him? ——I'll tell him all.

这个怎么用？

How to use this?

4. 关于钱的读法   guānyú qián de dúfǎ

"Kuài" is often used in oral language. For example:

两块三 ——2.3元 ——两元三

two yuan and three jiao

一百零四块 ——104元

one hundred and four yuan

Chinese Crash Course

两百六十块零五毛 ——260.5元

two hundred and sixty yuan and five jiao

Exercises

一 用适当的疑问词对划线部分提问 Use proper interrogative words to question about the underlined parts.

1. 那三个英国人是<u>坐地铁</u>来的。
   (   )?
2. 航空邮寄要<u>三百四十块钱</u>。
   (   )?
3. 带<u>身份证</u>可以取邮件。
   (   )?
4. <u>带身份证</u>可以取邮件。
   (   )?
5. 她去<u>邮局</u>办理快递业务。
   (   )?
6. 她去邮局办理<u>快递业务</u>。
   (   )?

二 选择 Choose the correct answers.

1. 我去邮局(　)邮件。
   A 要　　　　B 带　　　　C 称　　　　D 取

Lesson Twelve Do you want to post it by air mail or ordinary mail?

2. "108元"读作( )。

　A 一百八　　　B 一百八元　　C 一百八块　　D 一百零八块

3. 二百二十块零三毛是( )。

　A 20020.3元　　B 220.3元　　C 2203元　　D 223元

三　选词填空　Fill in the blanks with the proper words.

　　办理　　用　　航空邮寄　　重量　　着急　　寄　　取

1. 上课时我不喜欢( )词典。
2. 这个邮件的( )是多少？
3. 这个业务请到邮局去( )。
4. 这几本书是从哪里( )来的？
5. 请你不要( )，我们很快就会办理。
6. 我去李老师那里( )HSK的成绩单。
7. ( )当然要贵一点儿。

Supplementary Words

1. 包裹　　　bāoguǒ　　　名(n.)　　　package
2. 挂号信　　guàhàoxìn　　名(n.)　　　registered letter
3. 代取　　　dài qǔ　　　　　　　　　take on behalf of the owner
4. 邮政　　　yóuzhèng　　名(n.)　　　post
5. 保险费　　bǎoxiǎnfèi　　名(n.)　　　insurance premium

Chinese Crash Course

6. 回执	huízhí	名 (n.)		receipt
7. 公斤	gōngjīn	量 (mw)		kilogram
8. 克	kè	量 (mw)		gram
9. 日期	rìqī	名 (n.)		date
10. 到达	dàodá	动 (v.)		arrive
11. 找钱	zhǎo qián			make changes

Related Sentences

1. 请给我看一下您的身份证。
   Qǐng gěi wǒ kàn yíxià nín de shēnfènzhèng.
   Please show me your ID card.

2. 我是代别人取包裹的。
   Wǒ shì dài biéren qǔ bāoguǒ de.
   I take the package for someone else.

3. 请在这里签上名字。
   Qǐng zài zhèli qiānshang míngzi.
   Sign your name here, please.

4. 大概一个星期可以寄到。
   Dàgài yí ge xīngqī kěyǐ jìdào.
   It will arrive in one week.

5. 请收好您的回执单。
   Qǐng shōuhǎo nín de huízhídān.
   Please keep your receipt.

第 13 课 请把这些美元存到信用卡里。
Dì Shísān Kè Qǐng bǎ zhèxiē měiyuán cúndào xìnyòngkǎ li.

Lesson Thirteen   Please deposit these US dollars in the credit card.

Sentence Patterns

1. 请在6号窗口办理外汇业务。
   Qǐng zài liù hào chuāngkǒu bànlǐ wàihuì yèwù.
   Please do the foreign exchange business at Window No. 6.

2. 我想把这些美元换成人民币。
   Wǒ xiǎng bǎ zhèxiē měiyuán huànchéng rénmínbì.
   I want to exchange these US dollars for RMB.

3. 请输入密码。
   Qǐng shūrù mìmǎ.
   Input your code, please.

4. 只有中国银行办理这个业务吗?
   Zhǐyǒu Zhōngguó Yínháng bànlǐ zhège yèwù ma?
   Does only the Bank of China do this business?

5. 不一定。别的银行也可以。
   Bù yídìng. Bié de yínháng yě kěyǐ.
   I'm not sure. Other banks may also have such service.

Zhè zhāng xìnyòngkǎ zài hěn duō guójiā dōu kěyǐ yòng.
6. 这张信用卡在很多国家都可以用。

This credit card can be used in many countries.

Qǐng bǎ zhèxiē měiyuán cúndào xìnyòngkǎ li.
7. 请把这些美元存到信用卡里。

Please deposit these dollars in the credit card.

Zhèxiē shì yíwàn yuán zhěng, qǐng shǔ yíxià.
8. 这些是一万元整,请数一下。

These are ten thousand yuan full. Please count them.

Méi cuò!
9. 没错!

It's right!

Qǐng zài zhèli qiānmíng.
10. 请在这里签名。

Sign your name here, please.

Dialogues

Qǐngwèn, wǒ xiǎng huànqián, zài nǎge chuāngkǒu bànlǐ?
A: 请问,我想换钱,在哪个窗口办理?

Excuse me, I would like to change some money. At which window can I do this?

Lesson Thirteen Please deposit these US dollars in the credit card.

B: Zài wàihuì chuāngkǒu bànlǐ, jiù shì liù hào chuāngkǒu.
在外汇窗口办理，就是6号窗口。

You can do this at the foreign exchange window, No. 6.

A: Wǒ yào bǎ zhè zhāng cúnzhé li de měiyuán dōu huànchéng rénmínbì.
我要把这张存折里的美元都换成人民币。

I would like to change the US dollars in this deposit book into RMB.

B: Hǎo de. Qǐng shūrù mìmǎ.
好的。请输入密码。

OK, input your code please.

A: Qǐngwèn wàihuì páijià zài nǎr?
请问外汇牌价在哪儿？

Excuse me, where is the foreign exchange rate?

B：Jiù zài nàbiān de dà píngmù shang.
就 在 那 边 的 大 屏 幕 上。

It's shown on the big screen there.

A：Bié de yínháng yě bànlǐ wàihuì yèwù ma?
别 的 银 行 也 办 理 外 汇 业 务 吗？

Do other banks also do foreign exchange business?

B：Bié de yínháng yě bànlǐ yìbān de wàibì chǔxù yèwù.
别 的 银 行 也 办 理 一 般 的 外 币 储 蓄 业 务。

Other banks also do the ordinary foreign exchange deposit business.

A：Wàibì duìhuàn yèwù yě yǒu ma?
外 币 兑 换 业 务 也 有 吗？

Do they also have the foreign currency exchange business?

B：Duì.
对。

Yes.

A：Wǒ xiǎng kāi yí ge huóqī cúnzhé, zài bàn yì zhāng xìnyòngkǎ.
我 想 开 一 个 活 期 存 折，再 办 一 张 信 用 卡。

I would like to open a current deposit account and a credit card.

Lesson Thirteen   Please deposit these US dollars in the credit card.

B: Qǐng tián yíxià zhè zhāng biǎo.
请 填 一 下 这 张 表。

Please fill in this form.

A: Gōngshāng Yínháng de xìnyòngkǎ zài bié de guójiā kěyǐ yòng ma?
工 商 银 行 的 信 用 卡 在 别 的 国 家 可 以 用 吗？

Can the credit card of Industrial and Commercial Bank of China be used in other countries?

B: Hěn duō guójiā dōu kěyǐ yòng.
很 多 国 家 都 可 以 用。

You can use it in many other countries.

A: Qǐng bǎ zhèxiē rénmínbì cúndào zhè zhāng cúnzhé li,
请 把 这 些 人 民 币 存 到 这 张 存 折 里，

bǎ　　zhèxiē　měiyuán　cúndào　　xìnyòngkǎ　　li.
把 这 些 美 元 存 到 信 用 卡 里。

Please deposit these RMB in this deposit book and these dollars in the credit card.

Hǎo. Wǒ shǔ　yíxià.
B：好。我 数 一 下。

OK, let me count them.

Rénmínbì　　shì　liùqiān　sānbǎi yuán, měiyuán　shì　yíwàn
A：人 民 币 是 六 千 三 百 元，美 元 是 一 万
yuán zhěng.
元 整。

They are six thousand and three hundred yuan and ten thousand US dollars full.

Méi cuò. Qǐng zài　zhèli　qiānmíng.
B：没 错。请 在 这 里 签 名。

Exactly. Please sign your name here.

Bànwánle　　ma?
A：办 完 了 吗？

Is that all?

Wánle,　zhè shì nín de　cúnzhé　hé kǎ, qǐng shōuhǎo.
B：完 了，这 是 您 的 存 折 和 卡，请 收 好。

Yes. These are your bankbook and credit card, please.

Lesson Thirteen   Please deposit these US dollars in the credit card.

New Words

1.	窗口	chuāngkǒu	名 (n.)	window
2.	外汇	wàihuì	名 (n.)	foreign exchange
3.	把	bǎ	介 (prep.)	used in the "把" sentence
4.	存折	cúnzhé	名 (n.)	bankbook
5.	美元	měiyuán	名 (n.)	US dollar
6.	成	chéng	动 (v.)	become
7.	人民币	rénmínbì	名 (n.)	RMB
8.	输入	shūrù	动 (v.)	input
9.	密码	mìmǎ	名 (n.)	code
10.	牌价	páijià	名 (n.)	quotation
11.	屏幕	píngmù	名 (n.)	screen
12.	别的	bié de		other
13.	外币	wàibì	名 (n.)	foreign currency
14.	储蓄	chǔxì	动 (v.)	deposit
15.	兑换	duìhuàn	动 (v.)	exchange
16.	活期	huóqī	形 (adj.)	current
17.	办	bàn	动 (v.)	do
18.	信用卡	xìnyòngkǎ	名 (n.)	credit card

Chinese Crash Course

19.	国家	guójiā	名 (n.)	country
20.	用	yòng	动 (v.)	use
21.	存	cún	动 (v.)	put, deposit
22.	数	shǔ	动 (v.)	count
23.	千	qiān	数 (num.)	thousand
24.	万	wàn	数 (num.)	ten thousand
25.	整	zhěng	形 (adj.)	whole
26.	错	cuò	形 (adj.)	wrong
27.	签名	qiān//míng	动 (v.)	sign one's name
28.	完	wán	形 (adj.)	finished

Proper Nouns

1. 中国银行   Zhōngguó Yínháng   Bank of China
2. 中国工商银行 Zhōngguó Gōngshāng Yínháng   Industrial and Commercial Bank of China

Lesson Thirteen   Please deposit these US dollars in the credit card.

Annotations

1. 把美元换成人民币   *bǎ měiyuán huànchéng rénmínbì*

This is the typical pattern of the "bǎ" sentence in Chinese. The structure is "bǎ +object +verb +complement". "Chéng" is the complement of "huàn". This kind of sentence is used to emphasize the result and effect that the verb exerts on the object.

2. 别(的)   *bié (de)*

"Bié" here means other. For example:

别人都走了,只有我和他在这里。

Others had gone. Only he and I were here.

我只买了一件上衣,别的没有买。

I only bought a jacket.

这些钱存银行里,别的钱买东西吧。

Put this money in the bank and use other money for shopping.

3. 存折里/信用卡里   *cúnzhé li / xìnyòngkǎ li*

"Lǐ" is a noun of locality and is often used together with other nouns to form noun phrases. For example:

我们在书店里见面了。

We met each other in the bookshop.

我在手机里存了这个电话号码。

I put this phone number in my mobile phone.

词典里没有这个生词。

This new word can not be found in the dictionary.

4. 一万元整　　*yíwàn yuán zhěng*

"Zhěng" indicates a whole number and there is no oddment after the number. For example:

我要整钱,不要零钱。

I want the whole money, not the changes.

参加的有100人整,不要别人了。

There are one hundred participants, and don't need more.

这件衣服的价格是一千元整。

The price of this garment is one thousand whole.

5. 没错　　*méi cuò*

Equivalent to "duì","tóngyì" in oral language, it is often used as a simple answer or to echo others' words.

6. "百、千、万"的称数法　　*"bǎi、qiān、wàn" de chēngshùfǎ*

The way of reading "bǎi, qiān, wàn".

3,000	三千	three thousand
3,020	三千零二十	three thousand and twenty
3,200	三千二(百)	three thousand and two hundred
3,260	三千二百六	three thousand two hundred and sixty

Lesson Thirteen   Please deposit these US dollars in the credit card.

100,000	十万	one hundred thousand
130,000	十三万	one hundred and thirty thousand
22,000	两万二(千)	twenty-two thousand
22,220	两万二千二百二十	twenty-two thousand two hundred and twenty

Exercises

一　填空　Fill in the blanks with the proper words.

1. 我想(　　)一个存折,再办一(　　)信用卡。
2. 请把这些美元(　　)到这张存折(　　)。
3. 屏幕上有今天的外汇(　　)。
4. 这张信用卡在别的国家也可以(　　)。
5. 您要换(　　)还是美元?
6. 请(　　)密码。
7. 请问您取钱还是(　　)?

二　请读出下列数字　Please read the numbers below aloud.

　　23,330　　9,800　　8,705　　89,050

三　请写出下列数字　Please write out the following numbers in Arabic numerals.

　　五万三　　六百零六　　九万零三百　　七千零六十

四 请把下面的词连成句子　Please rearrange the following words into sentences.

1. 美元　　把　　　换成　　　请　　　人民币

2. 信用卡　这些钱　存到　　　里　　　把

3. 这家　　办理　　银行　　　外币储蓄　业务

4. 这张　　了　　　里　　　　没有钱　　信用卡

Supplementary Words

1. 余额	yú'é	名 (n.)	balance
2. 利息	lìxī	名 (n.)	interest
3. 取款	qǔ kuǎn		withdraw money
4. 自动取款机	zìdòng qǔkuǎnjī		Automatic Teller Machine (ATM)
5. 挂失	guà//shī	动 (v.)	report the loss of sth.
6. 中国农业银行	Zhōngguó Nóngyè Yínháng	专名 (pn)	Agricultural Bank of China
7. 国有银行	guóyǒu yínháng		state-owned bank

Lesson Thirteen Please deposit these US dollars in the credit card.

8. 私人银行	sīrén yínháng	动 (v.)	private bank
9. 澳元	àoyuán	名 (n.)	Australian dollar
10. 日元	rìyuán	名 (n.)	yen
11. 德国马克	Déguó mǎkè	名 (n.)	Deutschmark

 ## Related Sentences

1. 现在人民币对美元的比率是多少?
   Xiànzài rénmínbì duì měiyuán de bǐlǜ shì duōshao?
   What's the exchange rate between RMB and US dollar?

2. 中国有四大国有银行。
   Zhōngguó yǒu sì dà guóyǒu yínháng.
   China has four big state-owned banks.

3. 在中国也有很多外国银行和私人银行。
   Zài Zhōngguó yě yǒu hěn duō wàiguó yínháng hé sīrén yínháng.
   There are also many foreign banks and private banks in China.

4. 这些信用卡都有银联标志。
   Zhèxiē xìnyòngkǎ dōu yǒu Yínlián biāozhì.
   These credit cards all have the logo of bank network.

5. 我忘了存折的密码,请问怎么办?
   Wǒ wàngle cúnzhé de mìmǎ, qǐngwèn zěnme bàn?
   I forget the code of the bankbook. What can I do?

Chinese Crash Course

6. 这张信用卡只能在中国用。

   Zhè zhāng xìnyòngkǎ zhǐ néng zài Zhōngguó yòng.

   This credit card can only be used in China.

第 14 课 我喜欢太极拳和成龙的电影。
Dì Shísì Kè Wǒ xǐhuan tàijíquán hé Chéng Lóng de diànyǐng.

Lesson Fourteen I like shadow boxing and the movies of Jackie Chan.

Sentence Patterns

1. 你的爱好是什么？
   Nǐ de àihào shì shénme?
   What's your hobby?

2. 我爱好运动。
   Wǒ àihào yùndòng.
   I like sports.

3. 你不是喜欢中国功夫吗？
   Nǐ bú shì xǐhuan Zhōngguó gōngfu ma?
   Don't you like Chinese kungfu?

4. 这个对我不合适。
   Zhège duì wǒ bù héshì.
   It is not fit for me.

5. 我喜欢成龙的电影。
   Wǒ xǐhuan Chéng Lóng de diànyǐng.
   I like the movies of Jackie Chan.

Chinese Crash Course

6. Rúguǒ nǐ duì Zhōngguó gōngfu yǒu xìngqù, jiù qù shìshi ba.
如果你对中国功夫有兴趣，就去试试吧。

Have a try if you are interested in Chinese Kungfu.

7. Wǒ yào tīng yīnyuè le.
我要听音乐了。

I'm going to listen to the music.

8. Tāmen zài zuò shénme ne?
他们在做什么呢?

What are they doing?

9. Tāmen zhèngzài kàn zúqiú bǐsài.
他们正在看足球比赛。

They are watching the football match.

10. Tài yǒu yìsi le!
太有意思了!

How interesting it is!

11. Méi yìsi, wǒ zuì tǎoyàn zúqiú le!
没意思，我最讨厌足球了!

It isn't interesting. I dislike football most!

Lesson Fourteen I like shadow boxing and the movies of Jackie Chan.

Dialogues

A: Dàwèi, nǐ àihào shénme?
大卫，你爱好什么？

What's your hobby, David?

B: Wǒ àihào yùndòng. Nǐ ne?
我爱好运动。你呢？

I like sports. What about you?

A: Wǒ zuì xǐhuan Zhōngguó de tàijíquán le, wǒ xiànzài shì tàijíquánmí.
我最喜欢中国的太极拳了，我现在是太极拳迷。

I like Chinese shadow boxing most. I'm a fan of the shadow boxing now.

B：你不是电影迷吗？
Nǐ bú shì diànyǐngmí ma?

Aren't you a fan of movie?

A：太极拳太有意思了！现在我要练习太极拳。
Tàijíquán tài yǒu yìsi le! Xiànzài wǒ yào liànxí tàijíquán.

Shadow boxing is so interesting! I'm going to practice shadow boxing.

B：太极拳太慢了，对我不合适。
Tàijíquán tài màn le, duì wǒ bù héshì.

Shadow boxing is too slow. It doesn't suit me.

A：你不是喜欢中国功夫吗？
Nǐ bú shì xǐhuan Zhōngguó gōngfu ma?

Don't you like Chinese kungfu?

B：我喜欢成龙的电影，可是中国功夫太难了。
Wǒ xǐhuan Chéng Lóng de diànyǐng, kěshì Zhōngguó gōngfu tài nán le.

I like the movies of Jackie Chan but Chinese kungfu is too difficult.

A：如果你对中国功夫有兴趣，就去试试吧。
Rúguǒ nǐ duì Zhōngguó gōngfu yǒu xìngqù, jiù qù shì shi ba.

Have a try if you are interested in it.

Lesson Fourteen   I like shadow boxing and the movies of Jackie Chan.

B：Wǒ kǎolǜ yíxià, xiànzài wǒ yào tīng yīnyuè le.
　　我 考 虑 一 下，现 在 我 要 听 音 乐 了。

I would like to think it over and I'm going to listen to the music now.

A：Tāmen zài zuò shénme ne?
　　他 们 在 做 什 么 呢？

What are they doing?

B：Tāmen zhèngzài kàn diànshì.
　　他 们 正 在 看 电 视。

They are watching TV.

A：Zài kàn diànshìjù ma?
　　在 看 电 视 剧 吗？

Are they watching TV series?

B：Bú shì, tāmen zài kàn zúqiú bǐsài, tāmen dōu shì zúqiúmí.
　　不 是，他 们 在 看 足 球 比 赛，他 们 都 是 足 球 迷。

No. They are watching the football match. They are all football fans.

A：Méi yìsi, wǒ zuì tǎoyàn zúqiú le.
　　没 意 思，我 最 讨 厌 足 球 了。

It isn't interesting. I dislike the football most.

Chinese Crash Course

B：Rúguǒ nǐ shì nánrén, nǐ jiù huì xǐhuan zúqiú le.
如果你是男人，你就会喜欢足球了。

You would like it if you were a man.

A：Wǒ yào qù kàn diànshìjù le.
我要去看电视剧了。

I'm going to watch TV series.

B：Wǒ jiù tǎoyàn nàxiē "wǒ ài nǐ"、"nǐ ài wǒ" de dōngxi!
我就讨厌那些"我爱你"、"你爱我"的东西！

I hate the stuff full of "I love you", "You love me".

A：Měi ge rén dōu yǒu zìjǐ de àihào.
每个人都有自己的爱好。

Everyone has his own hobby.

Lesson Fourteen   I like shadow boxing and the movies of Jackie Chan.

B: Nà nǐ kàn diànshìjù, wǒ gēn tāmen yíkuàir kàn qiúsài.
那 你 看 电 视 剧， 我 跟 他 们 一 块 儿 看 球 赛。

Then you watch the TV play, and I watch the football match with them.

A: Hǎo ba!
好 吧！
OK!

New Words

1. 爱好	àihào	动、名 (v./n.)	like; hobby
2. 运动	yùndòng	动、名 (v./n.)	exercise; sport
3. 太极拳	tàijíquán	名 (n.)	shadow boxing
4. 迷	mí	名、动 (n./v.)	fan; fascinate
5. 电影	diànyǐng	名 (n.)	movie
6. 练习	liànxí	动、名 (v./n.)	practice; practice
7. 功夫	gōngfu	名 (n.)	kungfu
8. 难	nán	形 (adj.)	difficult
9. 如果	rúguǒ	连 (conj.)	if
10. 兴趣	xìngqù	名 (n.)	interest

Chinese Crash Course

11. 考虑	kǎolǜ	动 (v.)	think over
12. 听	tīng	动 (v.)	listen
13. 音乐	yīnyuè	名 (n.)	music
14. 做	zuò	动 (v.)	do
15. 正在	zhèngzài	副 (adv.)	be doing
16. 电视	diànshì	名 (n.)	television
17. 电视剧	diànshìjù	名 (n.)	TV series
18. 足球	zúqiú	名 (n.)	football
19. 比赛	bǐsài	动、名 (v./n.)	match; match
20. 讨厌	tǎoyàn	动 (v.)	dislike
21. 男人	nánrén	名 (n.)	man
22. 每	měi	代 (pron.)	each
23. 自己	zìjǐ	代 (pron.)	oneself
24. 球赛	qiúsài	名 (n.)	ball game

Proper Noun

成龙	Chéng Lóng	Jackie Chan

Lesson Fourteen I like shadow boxing and the movies of Jackie Chan.

Annotations

1. 你不是电影迷吗？/ 你不是喜欢中国功夫吗？

Nǐ bú shì diànyǐngmí ma? / Nǐ bú shì xǐhuan Zhōngguó gōngfu ma?

"Bú shì……ma" is a rhetorical question which requires no answer. The speaker is emphasizing the fact which is obviously a truth.

他不是韩国人吗？

Isn't he Korean?

你不是在学习汉语吗？

Aren't you learning Chinese?

这不是你的电话号码吗？

Isn't this your telephone number?

2. 对我不合适/对中国功夫感兴趣

duì wǒ bù héshì / duì Zhōngguó gōngfu gǎn xìngqù

"Duì" is a preposition here introducing the person or the thing concerned. And it is equivalent to "duìyú". For example:

他对我说：" 麻烦你了。"

He said to me: "Sorry for making you so much trouble."

我对学习汉语有兴趣。

I am very interested in learning Chinese.

他女朋友对他非常好。

His girlfriend treats him very well.

3. 如果……, 就……　　*Rúguǒ……, jiù……*

"Rúguǒ" is a conjunction. It indicates a hypothetical condition and is always echoed with "jiù". Sometimes, "jiù" could be ommitted. For example:

如果你能便宜一点儿,我就买。

I will buy it if you can make it a little cheaper.

如果我不在房间,你就打我的手机。

If I'm not in the room, you can call my mobile phone.

如果你不去,我也不去了。

If you don't go, I won't either.

4. 他们在做什么呢?　　*Tāmen zài zuò shénme ne?*

"Zài" and "zhèngzài" are adverbs that indicate an action is being done. We can just use the particle "ne" in oral language. Their negative forms are "méi" or "méiyou". "Méiyou" can be used as a simple reply. For example:

我们正在上课呢。

We are having classes.

我听音乐呢。

I'm listening to the music.

他在看电视。

He is watching TV.

Lesson Fourteen   I like shadow boxing and the movies of Jackie Chan.

你在看书吗? ——没有,我在看DVD。
Are you reading books? ——No. I'm watching DVD.

Exercises

一 完成句子 Complete the following sentences.

1. 王先生:你们正在做什么?
   大　卫:我们(　　　　　)呢。

2. 艾玛:昨天晚上10点你们在做什么呢?
   铃木:(　　　　　　)。

3. 王先生:艾玛去找你的时候你在做什么?
   大　卫:(　　　　　)。

4. 如果你喜欢太极拳,(　　　　　　)。

5. 如果你爱他,你就(　　　　　　)。

6. 我最讨厌(　　　　)。

7. 我最大的爱好是(　　　　　)。

8. 我最喜欢(　　　　)的电影和(　　　　)的音乐。

9. 我对(　　　　)很有兴趣。

二 选择 Choose the correct answers.

1. 我(　　)足球没兴趣。
   A 在　　　B 正在　　　C 对　　　D 给

2. 他们(　　)看成龙的电影呢。
   A 正在　　　B 没　　　C 不　　　D 就要

3. (　　)上课了,我们快走吧!

　　A 对　　　　B 正在　　　C 在　　　　D 快要

4. 这个电视剧最(　　　　),我真不想看。

　　A 有意思　　B 有意思极了　C 难　　　　D 没意思

5. 汉语很(　　)吗?

　　A 难　　　　B 兴趣　　　C 慢　　　　D 爱好

6. 他(　　)有女朋友吗?为什么还要找女朋友?

　　A 不是　　　B 是　　　　C 以前　　　D 要

7. 如果你不喜欢看电视剧,(　　　　)听音乐吧。

　　A 去就　　　B 就你去　　C 你就去　　D 你去就

8. 我对练习功夫(　　　　)。

　　A 没有意思　B 有意思　　C 没有兴趣　D 兴趣

9. 他们都是足球(　　　)。

　　A 了　　　　B 迷　　　　C 比赛　　　D 呢

10. 你真(　　)我吗?

　　A 爱　　　　B 爱好　　　C 兴趣　　　D 对

Supplementary Words

1. 篮球	lánqiú	名 (n.)	basketball
2. 乒乓球	pīngpāngqiú	名 (n.)	ping-pong
3. 羽毛球	yǔmáoqiú	名 (n.)	badminton
4. 网球	wǎngqiú	名 (n.)	tennis

Lesson Fourteen I like shadow boxing and the movies of Jackie Chan.

5. 高手	gāoshǒu	名 (n.)	master hand
6. 滑雪	huáxuě	动、名 (v./n.)	ski; skiing
7. 游泳	yóuyǒng	动、名 (v./n.)	swim; swimming
8. 小说	xiǎoshuō	名 (n.)	novel
9. 文学	wénxué	名 (n.)	literature

 **Related Sentences**

1. 我喜欢打篮球和乒乓球。
   Wǒ xǐhuan dǎ lánqiú hé pīngpāngqiú.
   I like to play basketball and ping-pong.
2. 他是网球高手。
   Tā shì wǎngqiú gāoshǒu.
   He is a master hand of tennis.
3. 我们这里有羽毛球馆。
   Wǒmen zhèlǐ yǒu yǔmáoqiúguǎn.
   We have a badminton gymnasium here.
4. 冬天这里有很多人来滑雪。
   Dōngtiān zhèlǐ yǒu hěn duō rén lái huáxuě.
   Many people come here to go skiing in winter.
5. 他是这次游泳比赛的冠军。
   Tā shì zhè cì yóuyǒng bǐsài de guànjūn.
   He is the champion of this swimming contest.

Chinese Crash Course

6. 我有时间的时候就读小说。

    Wǒ yǒu shíjiān de shíhou jiù dú xiǎoshuō.

    I read novels when I have time.

7. 他们都是文学爱好者。

    Tāmen dōu shì wénxué àihàozhě.

    They are all lovers of literature.

第 15 课 医生，我肚子特别疼！
Dì Shíwǔ Kè Yīshēng, wǒ dùzi tèbié téng!

Lesson Fifteen Doctor, I have a bad stomachache!

Sentence Patterns

1. 我今天觉得特别不舒服。
   Wǒ jīntiān juéde tèbié bù shūfu.

   I feel extremely uncomfortable today.

2. 有一点儿发烧，还拉肚子。
   Yǒu yìdiǎnr fāshāo, hái lā dùzi.

   I've got a little fever and loose bowels.

3. 现在越来越难受了。
   Xiànzài yuè lái yuè nánshòu le.

   I feel worse and worse now.

4. 先量一下体温。
   Xiān liáng yíxià tǐwēn.

   Take your temperature first.

5. 我给你开一点儿药。
   Wǒ gěi nǐ kāi yìdiǎnr yào.

   I will give you some medicine.

6. 一天三次，每次两片。
   Yì tiān sān cì, měi cì liǎng piàn.

   You should take it three times a day and two pills each time.

Chinese Crash Course

       Bié dānxīn!
7. 别 担 心！

Don't worry!

Dialogues

    Wǒ jīntiān juéde tèbié bù shūfu.
A: 我 今 天 觉 得 特 别 不 舒 服。

I feel extremely uncomfortable today.

    Shì bu shì bìng le? Fāshāo háishi wèikǒu bù hǎo?
B: 是 不 是 病 了？发 烧 还 是 胃 口 不 好？

Are you sick? Do you have a fever or a bad appetite?

Lesson Fifteen Doctor, I have a bad stomachache!

A: Yǒu yìdiǎnr fāshāo, hái lā le jǐ cì dùzi.
有一点儿发烧，还拉了几次肚子。

I've got a little fever and had bouts of diarrhea.

B: Nà wǒmen qù yīyuàn ba, rúguǒ yánzhòng le jiù máfan le.
那我们去医院吧，如果严重了就麻烦了。

Well, let's go to the hospital. It will cause a lot of trouble if it gets worse.

A: Wǒ yǐwéi shì gǎnmào le, xiànzài yuè lái yuè nánshòu le.
我以为是感冒了，现在越来越难受了。

I thought that I caught a cold. But I feel worse and worse now.

B: Zhǐhǎo qù kàn yīshēng le.
只好去看医生了。

So I have to go to see a doctor.

A: Zěnme le? Nǎli bù shūfu?
怎么了？哪里不舒服？

What's wrong with you? Do you feel uncomfortable?

B: Fāshāo le, hái lā dùzi.
发烧了，还拉肚子。

I've got a fever and loose bowels.

A: Shénme shíhou kāishǐ fāshāo de? Lā dùzi lā le
什么时候开始发烧的？拉肚子拉了

duō cháng shíjiān le?
多 长 时 间 了？

Since when did you have a fever and loose bowels?

B：Zuótiān wǎnshang kāishǐ dùzi jiù tèbié téng, jīntiān zǎo-
昨 天 晚 上 开 始 肚 子 就 特 别 疼， 今 天 早
shang fā de shāo.
上 发 的 烧。

I began to have a bad stomachache last night. And I got a fever this morning.

A：Xiān liáng yíxià tǐwēn.
先 量 一 下 体 温。

Take your temperature first.

(guòle yíhuìr)
(过 了 一 会 儿)

(a moment later)

Lesson Fifteen Doctor, I have a bad stomachache!

A: Nǐ chīguo shénme bù gānjìng de dōngxi ma?
你 吃 过 什 么 不 干 净 的 东 西 吗?

Did you eat something not clean?

B: Zuótiān gēn péngyou chī de yángròuchuàn, hēle diǎnr píjiǔ.
昨 天 跟 朋 友 吃 的 羊 肉 串, 喝 了 点 儿 啤 酒。

I ate some mutton kababs and drunk some beer with my friends.

A: Ěxīn ma? Ǒutùguo ma?
恶 心 吗? 呕 吐 过 吗?

Did you feel like vomiting?

B: Bù ěxīn, yě méiyou ǒutù.
不 恶 心, 也 没 有 呕 吐。

No, I didn't.

A: Yídìng shì yángròuchuàn de wèntí. Wǒ gěi nǐ kāi yìdiǎnr yào.
一 定 是 羊 肉 串 的 问 题。 我 给 你 开 一 点 儿 药。

There must be something wrong with the mutton kababs. I will give you some medicine.

B: Zhè yào zěnme chī?
这 药 怎 么 吃?

How to take it?

A: Yī tiān sān cì, měi cì liǎng piàn.
一 天 三 次, 每 次 两 片。

Take this medicine three times a day and two pills each time.

Chinese Crash Course

Xièxie dàifu.
B：谢 谢 大 夫。
Thank you.

Huíqu ba, bié dānxīn! Rúguǒ yánzhòng de huà zài guòlai.
A：回 去 吧，别 担 心！如果 严 重 的 话 再 过 来。
Don't worry! If it gets worse, please come back again.

New Words

1.	舒服	shūfu	形 (adj.)	comfortable
2.	病	bìng	名 (n.)	sickness
3.	发烧	fā//shāo	动 (v.)	have a fever
4.	胃口	wèikǒu	名 (n.)	appetite
5.	拉肚子	lā dùzi		have loose bowels
6.	医院	yīyuàn	名 (n.)	hospital
7.	严重	yánzhòng	形 (adj.)	serious
8.	以为	yǐwéi	动 (v.)	think
9.	感冒	gǎnmào	动 (v.)	catch a cold
10.	越来越	yuè lái yuè		more
11.	难受	nánshòu	形 (adj.)	feel ill
12.	只好	zhǐhǎo	副 (adv.)	have to
13.	医生	yīshēng	名 (n.)	doctor

Lesson Fifteen Doctor, I have a bad stomachache!

14. 疼	téng	形	(adj.)	aching
15. 量	liáng	动	(v.)	measure
16. 体温	tǐwēn	名	(n.)	one's temperature
17. 干净	gānjìng	形	(adj.)	clean
18. 羊肉串	yángròuchuàn	名	(n.)	mutton kabab
19. 恶心	ěxīn	形	(adj.)	queasy
20. 呕吐	ǒutù	动	(v.)	vomit, throw up
21. 开药	kāi yào			prescribe some medicine
22. 药	yào	名	(n.)	medicine
23. 片	piàn	量	(mw)	pill
24. 大夫	dàifu	名	(n.)	doctor
25. 回去	huí//qù	动	(v.)	go back
26. 别	bié	副	(adv.)	don't
27. 担心	dān//xīn	动	(v.)	worry
28. 过来	guò//lai	动	(v.)	come back

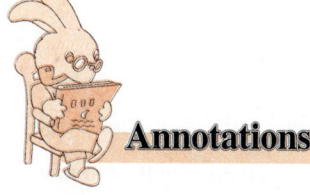

Annotations

1. **特别不舒服** *tèbié bù shūfu*

"Tèbié" is an adverb here, indicating a high degree. For example:

我特别爱吃辣的菜。

I like spicy dish very much.

我特别喜欢成龙的电影。

I like the movies of Jackie Chan very much.

这个比赛特别有意思。

This match is very interesting.

2. 是不是病了？　*Shì bu shì bìng le?*

"Shì bu shì" indicates that the speaker already has some understanding of the situation and he/she just wants to make sure. It can either be put at the beginning or at the end of a sentence. For example:

你是不是汉语老师？

Are you a Chinese teacher?

你来过两次中国,是不是？

You have been to China twice, haven't you?

那个医生特别好,是不是？

That doctor is very nice, isn't he?

3. 拉肚子/拉了几次肚子/拉肚子拉了多长时间

lā dùzi / lāle jǐ cì dùzi / lā dùzi lāle duō cháng shíjiān

The words like "shàngkè", "chī fàn" and "tīng yīnyuè" are the same in structure as "lā dùzi". They all follow the structure "verb + object". These phrases can be followed by a complement, a temporal word or a measure word. For example:

Lesson Fifteen Doctor, I have a bad stomachache!

我昨天听了两个小时的音乐。

I listened to the music for two hours yesterday.

吃饭吃了多长时间？

How long did you have your dinner?

The following are all ways to indicate the duration of time. For example:

他上课上了多长时间？

How long did he give classes?

他上了多长时间的课？

How long did he have the classes?

我等他等了一个小时。

I have waited for him for an hour.

我等了一个小时的车。

I have waited for the bus for one hour.

我等车等了一个小时。

I have waited for the bus for one hour.

4. **越来越难受**　　　yuè lái yuè nánshòu

"Yuè lái yuè+……" indicates the degree becomes deeper gradually. For example:

他的病越来越严重。

His illness is getting worse and worse.

车越来越快。

The bus is running faster and faster.

5. 拉了几次肚子   *lāle jǐ cì dùzi*

"Cì" is a measure word. It is used after a verb. For example:

他只上了两次课。

He only had two classes.

我去过三次图书馆。

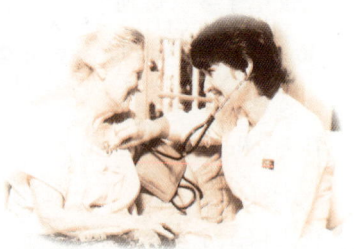

I have been to the library three times.

他来了几次。

He has been here several times.

6. 我以为是感冒了。   *Wǒ yǐwéi shì gǎnmào le.*

"Yǐwéi" indicates the conclusion made is contrary to the fact. For example:

我以为他今天能来。(但是他没有来)

I thought that he would have come here today. (But he didn't come.)

我以为他是韩国人。(但是他是日本人)

I thought he was Korean. (He is Japanese.)

我以为这个菜很好吃。(但是吃了以后觉得不好)

I thought the dish would be very delicious. (I find it not tasty after eating.)

7. 别担心   *bié dānxīn*

We have learned "biéren" and "bié de" in the preceding lessons. Here "bié" is an adverb that means to advise somebody to refrain from doing something. For example:

别喝酒了。

Don't drink any more.

Lesson Fifteen Doctor, I have a bad stomachache!

今天别去看电影了。

Don't go to see the film today.

别告诉他这件事情。

Don't tell him about this.

8. 再过来　　zài guòlai

Here "guò" is a verb. It is different from the verb termination "guo". "Lái" is a complement and it indicates the tendency of an action. For example:

我现在就过去,你等我。

I am coming now. Wait for me please.

他过来了,我们欢迎他。

He is coming. Let's welcome him.

两个小时以后你过来吧。

You can come here two hours later.

Exercises

一　按照例句用时间补语造句　Make sentences with time complement according to the example.

例句：拉肚子　两天——我拉了两天肚子。/我拉肚子拉了两天。

　　1. 看电影　一个半小时——

　　2. 听音乐　二十分钟——

3. 病　　一个星期——

4. 学汉语　三年——

5. 喝啤酒　四个小时——

二　完成对话　Complete the following dialogue.

医生：你哪里不舒服？

病人：(　　　　　　)。

医生：(　　　　)多长时间了？

病人：(　　　　　　)。

医生：别担心，我给你开点儿药。

病人：这药怎么吃？

医生：(　　　　　　)。

三　选词填空　Fill in the blanks with the proper words.

只好　　以为　　特别　　舒服　　别

担心　　严重　　越来越

1. 他这次考试的成绩(　　)好。

2. 我(　　)他是李小姐的男朋友。

3. (　　)吃这儿的羊肉串，太不干净了！

4. 我妈妈常常(　　)我的学习。

5. 我觉得在这个房间学习一定非常(　　)。

6. 地铁和公共汽车都没有了，我(　　)坐出租车了。

7. 肚子(　　)疼，我要去看医生了。

8. 他爸爸的病不(　　)，医生说很快就能好。

Lesson Fifteen Doctor, I have a bad stomachache!

Supplementary Words

1.	护士	hùshi	名 (n.)	nurse
2.	病人	bìngrén	名 (n.)	patient
3.	患者	huànzhě	名 (n.)	patient
4.	诊所	zhěnsuǒ	名 (n.)	clinic
5.	挂号	guà//hào	动 (v.)	register
6.	门诊	ménzhěn	名 (n.)	outpatient service
7.	急诊	jízhěn	动、名 (v./n.)	(give) emergency treatment
8.	住院	zhù//yuàn	动 (v.)	be in hospital; be hospitalized
9.	出院	chū//yuàn	动 (v.)	leave hospital
10.	手术	shǒushù	名 (n.)	operation
11.	外科	wàikē	名 (n.)	surgery
12.	内科	nèikē	名 (n.)	internal medicine

Chinese Crash Course

Related Sentences

1. 护士,请问外科在几楼?

   Hùshi, qǐngwèn wàikē zài jǐ lóu?

   Hello, which floor is the surgical department on, please?

2. 请问住院部在哪里?

   Qǐngwèn zhùyuànbù zài nǎli?

   Excuse me, where is the inpatient department?

3. 我来看一个病人。

   Wǒ lái kàn yí ge bìngrén.

   I come to see a patient.

4. 去照个 CT 吧。

   Qù zhào ge CT ba.

   Go to take a CT.

5. 你需要住院治疗。

   Nǐ xūyào zhùyuàn zhìliáo.

   You need to be in hospital to get treatment.

6. 手术要很长时间。

   Shǒushù yào hěn cháng shíjiān.

   It will take the doctors a long time to do the operation.

New Words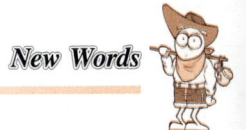

生 词

New Words

(Including Supplementary Words)

A

啊	a	(助)	*particle*	L6
爱	ài	(动)	love	L4
爱好	àihào	(动、名)	like; hobby	L14
爱情	àiqíng	(名)	love	L4
安排	ānpái	(动、名)	arrange; arrangement	L11-S
澳元	àoyuán	(名)	Australian dollar	L13-S

B

八	bā	(数)	eight	L5
把	bǎ	(介)	used in the "把" sentence	L13
爸爸	bàba	(名)	father	L4
白天	báitiān	(名)	daytime	L11
百	bǎi	(数)	hundred	L12
百货	bǎihuò	(名)	general merchandise	L10-S
办	bàn	(动)	do	L13
办理	bànlǐ	(动)	do	L12
半	bàn	(形)	half	L5

Chinese Crash Course

包	bāo	（名）	bag	L3
包裹	bāoguǒ	（名）	package	L12-S
包间/单间	bāojiān/dānjiān	（名）	separate room (rented in a restaurant)	L7-S
保险费	bǎoxiǎnfèi	（名）	insurance premium	L12-S
报名	bào//míng	（动）	sign up	L11
北	běi	（名）	north	L3-S
本	běn	（量）	*measure word*	L3
比赛	bǐsài	（动、名）	match; match	L14
笔	bǐ	（名）	pen	L3
笔记本	bǐjìběn	（名）	notebook	L2
笔记本电脑	bǐjìběn diànnǎo		laptop computer	L2
边	biān	（名）	side	L2
表	biǎo	（名）	table, form	L12
别	bié	（副）	don't	L15
别的	bié de		other	L13
别人	biéren	（名）	other people	L3
宾馆	bīnguǎn	（名）	hotel	L3-S
病	bìng	（名）	sickness	L15
病人	bìngrén	（名）	patient	L15-S
不错	búcuò	（形）	good	L7
不客气	bú kèqi		You are welcome.	L2
不	bù	（副）	no	L1
不一定	bù yídìng		not sure	L9

New Words

C

才	cái	（副）	only	L10
菜	cài	（名）	dish	L7
菜谱	càipǔ	（名）	menu	L7
参加	cānjiā	（动）	take part in	L11
餐厅	cāntīng	（名）	restaurant	L7
查	chá	（动）	check	L8-S
差	chà	（动、形）	fall short of; inferior	L5
超市	chāoshì	（名）	supermarket	L2
炒菜	chǎocài	（名）	stir-fried dish	L7-S
称	chēng	（动）	weigh	L12
成	chéng	（动）	become	L13
成绩	chéngjì	（名）	score	L11
吃饭	chī fàn		have a meal	L2
迟到	chídào	（动）	be late	L5
出发	chūfā	（动）	start	L9
出去	chū//qù	（动）	be out	L8
出院	chū//yuàn	（动）	leave hospital	L15-S
出租车	chūzūchē	（名）	taxi	L9
储蓄	chǔxù	（动）	deposit	L13
穿	chuān	（动）	put on	L10
窗口	chuāngkǒu	（名）	window	L13
词典/辞典	cídiǎn/cídiǎn	（名）	dictionary	L2
次	cì	（量）	time	L8

从	cóng	(介)	from	L12
存	cún	(动)	put, deposit	L13
存折	cúnzhé	(名)	bankbook	L13
错	cuò	(形)	wrong	L13

D

打	dǎ	(动)	call	L8
打车	dǎ//chē	(动)	take a taxi	L9-S
打折	dǎ//zhé	(动)	discount	L10-S
大概	dàgài	(副)	probably	L12
大学	dàxué	(名)	university	L11
大夫	dàifu	(名)	doctor	L15
带	dài	(动)	take	L12
代取	dài qǔ		take on behalf of the owner	L12-S
担心	dān//xīn	(动)	worry	L15
但是	dànshì	(连)	but	L6
当然	dāngrán	(副)	certainly	L4
到	dào	(动)	arrive	L6
到达	dàodá	(动)	arrive	L12-S
德国马克	Déguó mǎkè	(名)	Deutschmark	L13-S
的	de	(助)	*partical*	L2
登记	dēngjì	(动)	check in	L11-S
等	děng	(动)	wait	L7

New Words

第	dì	(头)	prefix for ordinal numbers	L3
第一	dì yī		first	L3
地方	dìfang	(名)	place	L2
地铁	dìtiě	(名)	subway	L9
地铁站	dìtiězhàn	(名)	subway station	L9
地图	dìtú	(名)	map	L9
地址	dìzhǐ	(名)	address	L8-S
点	diǎn	(动)	order	L7
点/点钟	diǎn/diǎnzhōng	(量)	o'clock	L5
电话	diànhuà	(名)	telephone	L8
电脑	diànnǎo	(名)	computer	L2
电器	diànqì	(名)	electric appliance	L10-S
电视	diànshì	(名)	television	L14
电视剧	diànshìjù	(名)	TV series	L14
电影	diànyǐng	(名)	movie	L14
电子邮件	diànzǐ yóujiàn		e-mail	L8
东	dōng	(名)	east	L3-S
东北菜	Dōngběicài	(名)	Northeastern cuisine	L7-S
东西	dōngxi	(名)	thing	L3
都	dōu	(副)	all	L2
堵车(塞车)	dǔ//chē(sāi//chē)	(动)	traffic jam	L9-S
对	duì	(形)	right	L2
对不起	duìbuqǐ	(动)	excuse me	L3-S
兑换	duìhuàn	(动)	exchange	L13

Chinese Crash Course

多	duō	（形）	many	L1-S
多少钱	duōshao qián		how much	L10

E

恶心	ěxīn	（形）	queasy	L15
饿	è	（形）	hungry	L7
儿子	érzi	（名）	son	L4-S
二十	èrshí	（数）	twenty	L5

F

发	fā	（动）	send	L8
发票	fāpiào	（名）	invoice	L9-S
发烧	fā//shāo	（动）	have a fever	L15
翻译	fānyì	（动、名）	translate; interpreter	L11
饭店	fàndiàn	（名）	restaurant	L2
房间	fángjiān	（名）	room	L2-S
非常	fēicháng	（副）	very	L10
分/分钟	fēn/fēnzhōng	（量）	minute	L5
分机	fēnjī	（名）	extension	L8-S
分手	fēn//shǒu	（动）	part	L4
服务员	fúwùyuán	（名）	waiter	L7
服装	fúzhuāng	（名）	clothes	L10
辅导	fǔdǎo	（动）	tutor	L11

New Words

辅导班	fǔdǎobān	（名）	tutoring class	L11
附件	fùjiàn	（名）	appendix, accessory, attachment	L8-S
附近	fùjìn	（名）	neighborhood	L3

G

该/应该	gāi/yīnggāi	（助动）	should	L5
干净	gānjìng	（形）	clean	L15
感冒	gǎnmào	（动）	catch a cold	L15
刚刚	gānggāng	（副）	just	L10
高峰时间	gāofēng shíjiān		rush hour	L9-S
高手	gāoshǒu	（名）	master hand	L14-S
高兴	gāoxìng	（动）	glad, be happy	L1
告诉	gàosu	（动）	tell	L8
哥哥	gēge	（名）	elder brother	L4
个	gè	（量）	measure word	L3
给	gěi	（动、介）	give; for	L8
工作	gōngzuò	（名、动）	work; work	L8
公共汽车	gōnggòng qìchē		bus	L9
公共汽车站	gōnggòng qìchēzhàn		bus stop	L9-S
公斤	gōngjīn	（量）	kilogram	L12-S
公司	gōngsī	（名）	corporation	L8
功夫	gōngfu	（名）	kungfu	L14
宫保鸡丁	gōngbǎojīdīng	（名）	sauted chicken cubes with chilli and peanuts	L7-S

购物	gòu wù		go shopping	L10-S
姑娘	gūniang	(名)	girl	L4
挂号	guà//hào	(动)	register	L15-S
挂号信	guàhàoxìn	(名)	registered letter	L12-S
挂失	guà//shī	(动)	report the loss of sth.	L13-S
拐	guǎi	(动)	turn	L3
关照	guānzhào	(动)	look after	L1-S
广告	guǎnggào	(名)	advertisement	L11
逛	guàng	(动)	stroll	L10-S
贵	guì	(形)	expensive	L1
贵姓	guìxìng	(名)	your surname	L1
国	guó	(名)	country	L1
国家	guójiā	(名)	country	L13
国有银行	guóyǒu yínháng		state-owned bank	L13-S
果汁	guǒzhī	(名)	fruit juice	L7
过	guò	(动)	pass	L5
过来	guò//lái	(动)	come back	L15

H

还	hái	(副)	still	L7
还是	háishi	(连、副)	still	L9
孩子	háizi	(名)	child	L4-S
汉语	Hànyǔ	(名)	Chinese	L1

New Words

航空	hángkōng	（名）	air	L12
好	hǎo	（形）	good	L1
好吃	hǎochī	（形）	delicious	L7
号	hào	（名）	date	L5
号码	hàomǎ	（名）	number	L8
喝	hē	（动）	drink	L7
和	hé	（连、介）	and	L3
合适	héshì	（形）	fit; suit	L10
很	hěn	（副）	very	L1
红绿灯	hónglǜdēng	（名）	traffic light	L3
红烧排骨	hóngshāo páigǔ		pork ribs braised in soy sauce	L7
后来	hòulái	（名）	later	L4-S
后面	hòumian	（名）	back	L2-S
后天	hòutiān	（名）	the day after tomorrow	L5
互相	hùxiāng	（副）	each other	L1-S
护士	hùshi	（名）	nurse	L15-S
滑雪	huáxuě	（动、名）	ski; skiing	L14-S
化妆品	huàzhuāngpǐn	（名）	cosmetic	L10
欢迎	huānyíng	（动）	welcome	L1
环城铁路	huánchéng tiělù		railway round the city	L9-S
环境	huánjìng	（名）	environment	L7
换	huàn	（动）	change	L9
患者	huànzhě	（名）	patient	L15-S
回去	huí//qù	（动）	go back	L15

回执	huízhí	（名）	receipt	L12-S
会	huì	（动、助动）	can	L5
活期	huóqī	（形）	current	L13
火锅	huǒguō	（名）	hot pot	L7

J

机会	jīhuì	（名）	chance, opportunity	L11
极	jí	（副）	very	L11
急事	jí shì		something urgent	L9
急诊	jízhěn	（动、名）	(give) emergency treatment	L15-S
几	jǐ	（代）	several	L3
记住	jìzhù	（动）	remember	L8
家电	jiādiàn	（名）	household electric appliances	L10-S
价格	jiàgé	（名）	price	L10
价钱	jiàqián	（名）	price	L10-S
见	jiàn	（动）	meet	L6
见面	jiàn//miàn	（动）	meet	L6
件	jiàn	（量）	piece	L10
交	jiāo	（动）	hand in, pay	L11
交费	jiāo fèi		pay the fee	L11-S
交通	jiāotōng	（名）	traffic	L9-S
叫	jiào	（动）	be named	L1

New Words

教材	jiàocái	（名）	teaching material	L11
接	jiē	（动）	answer	L8
接收	jiēshōu	（动）	receive, accept	L8-S
接线员	jiēxiànyuán	（名）	operator	L8-S
结婚	jié//hūn	（动）	marry	L4
介绍	jièshào	（动）	introduce	L1-S
斤	jīn	（量）	half a kilogram	L7
今天	jīntiān	（名）	today	L5
进步	jìnbù	（动）	make progress	L11
九	jiǔ	（数）	nine	L5
酒吧	jiǔbā	（名）	bar	L7-S
酒水	jiǔshuǐ	（名）	beverages and alcohol	L7
就	jiù	（副）	just	L3
觉得	juéde	（动）	feel	L6

K

开	kāi	（动）	have	L5
开始	kāishǐ	（动）	start	L8
开学	kāi//xué	（动）	term begins	L11-S
开药	kāi yào		prescribe some medicine	L15
开业	kāi//yè	（动）	open	L10
看	kàn	（动）	look at	L4
考虑	kǎolǜ	（动）	think over	L14

考试	kǎoshì	（动、名）	test; test	L11
烤鸭	kǎoyā	（名）	roast duck	L7
可能	kěnéng	（副）	maybe	L11
可是	kěshì	（连）	but	L4
可以	kěyǐ	（助动）	can	L3
克	kè	（量）	gram	L12-S
课本	kèběn	（名）	textbook	L2
课程	kèchéng	（量）	course	L11-S
刻	kè	（量）	quarter	L5
空儿	kòngr	（名）	spare time	L6-S
口	kǒu	（量）	measure word	L4
口味	kǒuwèi	（名）	taste	L7
块	kuài	（量）	yuan	L12
快	kuài	（形）	quick	L5
快递	kuàidì	（名）	express delivery	L12
快乐	kuàilè	（形）	happy	L4-S
款式	kuǎnshì	（名）	style	L10-S

拉肚子	lā dùzi		have loose bowels	L15
辣	là	（形）	hot, spicy	L7
来	lái	（动）	come	L1
来不及	láibují	（动）	it's too late	L5
来得及	láidejí	（动）	there's still time	L5

New Words

来自	lái zì		come from	L1-S
篮球	lánqiú	（名）	basketball	L14-S
老地方	lǎo dìfang		old place	L6-S
老师	lǎoshī	（名）	teacher	L1
老样子	lǎo yàngzi		same as usual	L6-S
了	le	（助）	*particle*	L4
离	lí	（介、动）	from; depart	L9
离婚	lí//hūn	（动）	divorce	L4-S
里	lǐ	（名）	inside	L2
里程表	lǐchéngbiǎo	（名）	odometer	L9-S
礼品	lǐpǐn	（名）	present, gift	L10
利息	lìxī	（名）	interest	L13-S
联系	liánxì	（动）	contact	L8
练习	liànxí	（动、名）	practice; practice	L14
恋爱	liàn'ài	（动）	fall in love	L4
量	liáng	（动）	measure	L15
凉菜	liángcài	（名）	cold dish	L7-S
两	liǎng	（数）	two	L4
零	líng	（数）	zero	L12
领	lǐng	（动）	take	L11
领取	lǐngqǔ	（动）	draw, get	L12
六	liù	（数）	six	L5
楼	lóu	（名）	building	L3-S
楼	lóu	（名）	floor	L10
路	lù	（名）	road	L9

路口	lùkǒu	(名)	crossroad	L3

M

妈妈	māma	(名)	mother	L4
麻烦	máfan	(动、名)	trouble; trouble	L8
吗	ma	(助)	*modal particle*	L1
买	mǎi	(动)	buy	L10
买单	mǎidān	(动)	pay the bill	L7-S
满意	mǎnyì	(形)	satisfied	L10
慢	màn	(形)	slow	L9
忙	máng	(形、动)	busy; be busy with	L6
没	méi	(副)	no	L3
没问题	méi wèntí		no problem	L6
没(有)意思	méi (yǒu) yìsi		not interesting	L6-S
每	měi	(代)	each	L14
美元	měiyuán	(名)	US dollar	L13
妹妹	mèimei	(名)	younger sister	L4
门口	ménkǒu	(名)	gate	L2
门诊	ménzhěn	(名)	outpatient service	L15-S
们	men	(尾)	*suffix*	L1
迷	mí	(名、动)	fan; fascinate	L14
米	mǐ	(量)	meter	L3-S
密码	mìmǎ	(名)	code	L13
面包	miànbāo	(名)	bread	L7-S

New Words

面条	miàntiáo	(名)	noodle	L7
名字	míngzi	(名)	name	L1
明年	míngnián	(名)	next year	L4
明天	míngtiān	(名)	tomorrow	L5

N

哪	nǎ	(代)	which	L1
哪儿	nǎr	(代)	where	L2
那	nà	(代)	that	L2
男朋友	nánpéngyou	(名)	boyfriend	L4-S
男人	nánrén	(名)	man	L14
男式	nán shì		male style	L10
难	nán	(形)	difficult	L14
难受	nánshòu	(形)	feel ill	L15
呢	ne	(助)	*modal particle*	L1
内科	nèikē	(名)	internal medicine	L15-S
能	néng	(助动)	can	L9
你	nǐ	(代)	you	L1
你好	nǐ hǎo		hello	L1
年	nián	(名)	year	L4
年末	niánmò	(名)	end of the year	L5-S
您	nín	(代)	you (respectful form of "你")	L1
女	nǚ	(名)	woman	L4

Chinese Crash Course

女儿	nǚ'ér	(名)	daughter	L4-S
女孩	nǚhái	(名)	girl	L4
女朋友	nǚpéngyou	(名)	girlfriend	L4
女式	nǚ shì		female style	L10

O

哦	ò	(叹)	used to indicate realization or understanding	L8
呕吐	ǒutù	(动)	vomit, throw up	L15

P

牌价	páijià	(名)	quotation	L13
旁边	pángbiān	(名)	side, next to	L3
朋友	péngyou	(名)	friend	L6
啤酒	píjiǔ	(名)	beer	L7
便宜	piányi	(形)	cheap	L10
片	piàn	(量)	pill	L15
漂亮	piàoliang	(形)	beautiful, pretty	L4
乒乓球	pīngpāngqiú	(名)	ping-pong	L14-S
瓶	píng	(名、量)	bottle	L7
屏幕	píngmù	(名)	screen	L13
普通	pǔtōng	(形)	ordinary	L12

New Words

Q

妻子	qīzi	(名)	wife	L4-S
旗袍	qípáo	(名)	cheongsam	L10
起床	qǐ//chuáng	(动)	get up	L5
千	qiān	(数)	thousand	L13
签名	qiān//míng	(动)	sign one's name	L13
钱	qián	(名)	money	L3
前边	qiánbian	(名)	in front of	L2
轻松	qīngsōng	(形)	relaxed	L5
清楚	qīngchu	(形)	clear	L8-S
清淡	qīngdàn	(形)	light	L7-S
请	qǐng	(动)	please	L1-S
请客	qǐng//kè	(动)	invite somebody to dinner	L7-S
请问	qǐngwèn	(动)	excuse me	L1
球赛	qiúsài	(名)	ball game	L14
取	qǔ	(动)	take	L12
取款	qǔ kuǎn		withdraw money	L13-S
去	qù	(动)	go	L2
去年	qùnián	(名)	last year	L11

R

然后	ránhòu	（连）	then	L11
人	rén	（名）	person	L1
人民币	rénmínbì	（名）	RMB	L13
任课教师	rènkè jiàoshī		instructor	L11-S
认识	rènshi	（动）	know	L1
日期	rìqī	（名）	date	L12-S
日元	rìyuán	（名）	yen	L13-S
如果	rúguǒ	（连）	if	L14
入学	rù//xué	（动）	enroll	L11-S

S

商场	shāngchǎng	（名）	shop	L10
商店	shāngdiàn	（名）	store	L2-S
商品	shāngpǐn	（名）	commodity	L10-S
上车	shàng chē		get on the car	L9
上个月	shàng ge yuè		last month	L5-S
上课	shàng//kè	（动）	attend class	L5
上网	shàng//wǎng	（动）	get on the internet	L2-S
上午	shàngwǔ	（名）	morning	L6-S
上衣	shàngyī	（名）	coat	L10
稍	shāo	（副）	a little	L7

New Words

少	shǎo	(形)	few	L9
身份证	shēnfènzhèng	(名)	ID card	L12
什么	shénme	(代)	what	L1
生活	shēnghuó	(名、动)	life; live	L4
生活用品	shēnghuó yòngpǐn		daily necessities	L10-S
生日	shēngrì	(名)	birthday	L5
师傅	shīfu	(名)	master	L9
十	shí	(数)	ten	L5
时候	shíhou	(名)	time	L6
时间	shíjiān	(名)	time	L5
式	shì	(名)	style	L10
事	shì	(名)	thing	L5
试	shì	(动)	try on	L10
是	shì	(动)	be	L1
适合	shìhé	(动)	fit, suit	L7
收	shōu	(动)	receive	L8
手机	shǒujī	(名)	mobile phone	L8
手术	shǒushù	(名)	operation	L15-S
手续	shǒuxù	(名)	procedure	L11-S
售货员	shòuhuòyuán	(名)	salesperson	L10-S
书	shū	(名)	book	L3
书店	shūdiàn	(名)	bookstore	L2-S
蔬菜	shūcài	(名)	vegetable	L7-S
舒服	shūfu	(形)	comfortable	L15
输入	shūrù	(动)	input	L13

227 速成中文

Chinese Crash Course

数	shǔ	（动）	count	L13
刷卡	shuā//kǎ	（动）	pay with the credit card	L10-S
谁	shuí/shéi	（代）	who	L1
水饺/饺子	shuǐjiǎo/jiǎozi	（名）	dumpling	L7
水平	shuǐpíng	（名）	level	L11
水煮鱼	shuǐzhǔyú	（名）	boiled spicy fish slices	L7
说	shuō	（动）	speak	L11
私人银行	sīrén yínháng		private bank	L13-S
宿舍	sùshè	（名）	dormitory	L2-S
算账	suàn//zhàng	（动）	pay the bill	L7-S

他	tā	（代）	he, him	L1
她	tā	（代）	she, her	L1
太	tài	（副）	too	L5
太极拳	tàijíquán	（名）	shadow boxing	L14
糖醋鱼	tángcùyú	（名）	fish in sweet and sour sauce	L7-S
讨厌	tǎoyàn	（动）	dislike	L14
特色菜	tèsècài	（名）	special dish	L7-S
疼	téng	（形）	aching	L15
体温	tǐwēn	（名）	one's temperature	L15
填	tián	（动）	fill in	L12

New Words

条	tiáo	(量)	*measure word*	L9
听	tīng	(动)	listen	L14
通	tōng	(动)	connect	L8
通知	tōngzhī	(动、名)	give notice; notice	L12
通知单	tōngzhīdān	(名)	notification	L12
图书馆	túshūguǎn	(名)	library	L2

W

外币	wàibì	(名)	foreign currency	L13
外汇	wàihuì	(名)	foreign exchange	L13
外科	wàikē	(名)	surgery	L15-S
外语	wàiyǔ	(名)	foreign language	L11
完	wán	(形)	finished	L13
晚会	wǎnhuì	(名)	evening party	L5
晚上	wǎnshang	(名)	evening	L6
万	wàn	(数)	ten thousand	L13
王	Wáng	(名)	a surname	L1
往	wǎng	(动、介)	head; to	L3
网吧	wǎngbā	(名)	internet cafe	L2
网络	wǎngluò	(名)	network	L8
网球	wǎngqiú	(名)	tennis	L14-S
为什么	wèi shénme		why	L6
位	wèi	(量)	*measure word*	L8
胃口	wèikǒu	(名)	appetite	L15

Chinese Crash Course

喂	wèi	(叹)	hello	L8
文学	wénxué	(名)	literature	L14-S
问	wèn	(动)	ask	L1
问题	wèntí	(名)	problem	L6
我	wǒ	(代)	I	L1
我们	wǒmen	(代)	we, us	L1

X

西餐	xīcān	(名)	Western food	L7-S
习惯	xíguàn	(名、动)	habit; get used to	L7
喜欢	xǐhuan	(动)	like	L6
下	xià	(名)	next	L6
下车	xià chē		get off	L6
下个月	xià ge yuè		next month	L5-S
下午	xiàwǔ	(名)	afternoon	L6
下一站	xià yí zhàn		next stop	L9-S
先	xiān	(副)	first	L1-S
先生	xiānsheng	(名)	Mr.	L8
咸	xián	(形)	salty	L7-S
现金	xiànjīn	(名)	cash	L10-S
现在	xiànzài	(名)	now	L3
湘菜	Xiāngcài	(名)	Hunan cuisine	L7-S
想	xiǎng	(动)	want	L2
向	xiàng	(介)	to	L3-S

New Words

小说	xiǎoshuō	（名）	novel	L14-S
些	xiē	（量）	some	L2
写	xiě	（动）	write	L12
谢谢	xièxie	（动）	thank	L1
新	xīn	（形）	new	L4
信用卡	xìnyòngkǎ	（名）	credit card	L13
星期	xīngqī	（名）	week	L5
星期天/星期日	xīngqītiān/xīngqīrì	（名）	Sunday	L5
行	xíng	（形）	possible	L11
姓	xìng	（名、动）	surname; surname	L1
兴趣	xìngqù	（名）	interest	L14
幸福	xìngfú	（形）	happy	L4
休息	xiūxi	（动）	rest; have a break	L5
学费	xuéfèi	（名）	tuition	L11
学生	xuésheng	（名）	student	L1-S
学时	xuéshí	（名）	class period	L11-S
学习	xuéxí	（动）	study, learn	L11
学校	xuéxiào	（名）	school	L2

严重	yánzhòng	（形）	serious	L15
羊肉串	yángròuchuàn	（名）	mutton kabab	L15
样式	yàngshì	（名）	style	L10
药	yào	（名）	medicine	L15

Chinese Crash Course

要	yào	（助动）	need	L9
要……了	yào……le		be about to	L6
也	yě	（副）	also, too	L1
也许	yěxǔ	（副）	maybe	L8
业务	yèwù	（名）	business	L12
衣服	yīfu	（名）	clothes	L10
医生	yīshēng	（名）	doctor	L15
医院	yīyuàn	（名）	hospital	L15
一定	yídìng	（副）	must	L7
一会儿	yíhuìr	（数量）	for a while	L5
一块儿	yíkuàir	（副）	together	L10
以后	yǐhòu	（名）	after	L4-S
以前	yǐqián	（名）	before	L4
以为	yǐwéi	（动）	think	L15
已经	yǐjīng	（副）	already	L4
一般	yìbān	（形、副）	general; generally	L6-S
一边……一边……	yìbiān……yìbiān……		at the same time	L11
一点儿	yìdiǎnr	（数量）	a little	L7
一直	yìzhí	（副）	straight	L3-S
音乐	yīnyuè	（名）	music	L14
银行	yínháng	（名）	bank	L2
饮料	yǐnliào	（名）	drink	L7
英语	Yīngyǔ	（名）	English	L2
用	yòng	（动）	use	L13
优惠	yōuhuì	（动、形）	favor; favorable	L10-S

New Words

邮寄	yóujì	（动）	post	L12
邮件	yóujiàn	（名）	mail	L8
邮局	yóujú	（名）	post office	L2-S
邮箱	yóuxiāng	（名）	mailbox	L8
邮政	yóuzhèng	（名）	post	L12-S
油腻	yóunì	（形）	greasy	L7
游泳	yóuyǒng	（动、名）	swim; swimming	L14-S
友谊	yǒuyì	（名）	friendship	L9
有	yǒu	（动）	have	L3
有意思	yǒu yìsi		interesting	L6
又	yòu	（副）	as well	L10
右	yòu	（名）	right	L3
鱼香肉丝	yúxiāngròusī	（名）	fish-flavored shredded pork	L7-S
余额	yú'é	（名）	balance	L13-S
羽毛球	yǔmáoqiú	（名）	badminton	L14-S
元	yuán	（名）	yuan	L10
远	yuǎn	（形）	far	L9
约会	yuēhuì	（动、名）	date; date	L6-S
月	yuè	（名）	month	L5-S
月末	yuèmò	（名）	end of the month	L5-S
越来越	yuè lái yuè		more	L15
粤菜	Yuècài	（名）	Guangdong cuisine	L7-S
运动	yùndòng	（动、名）	exercise; sport	L14

Chinese Crash Course

Z

再	zài	(副)	again	L3
再见	zàijiàn	(动)	good-bye	L2
怎么	zěnme	(代)	how	L3-S
怎么样	zěnmeyàng	(代)	how about	L6
张	zhāng	(量)	piece	L12
丈夫	zhàngfu	(名)	husband	L4-S
着急	zháo//jí	(形)	anxious, worried	L12
找	zhǎo	(动)	find	L4
找钱	zhǎo qián		make changes	L12-S
照片(相片)	zhàopiàn(xiàngpiàn)	(名)	picture, photo	L4
照相机	zhàoxiàngjī	(名)	camera	L3
这	zhè	(代)	this	L2
着呢	zhene	(助)	used to indicate a state	L12
真	zhēn	(副)	really	L4
诊所	zhěnsuǒ	(名)	clinic	L15-S
整	zhěng	(形)	whole	L13
正常	zhèngcháng	(形)	normal	L8
正在	zhèngzài	(副)	be doing	L14
证件	zhèngjiàn	(名)	certificate	L12
支	zhī	(量)	*measure word*	L3
知道	zhīdào	(动)	know	L3
只	zhǐ	(副)	only	L9

New Words

只好	zhǐhǎo	(副)	have to	L15
中餐	zhōngcān	(名)	Chinese food	L7-S
中国菜	Zhōngguócài	(名)	Chinese cuisine	L7
中级	zhōngjí	(名)	intermediate	L11
中文	Zhōngwén	(名)	Chinese	L11
中午	zhōngwǔ	(名)	noon	L5-S
重量	zhòngliàng	(名)	weight	L12
周末	zhōumò	(名)	weekend	L5-S
主食	zhǔshí	(名)	staple food	L7
住院	zhù//yuàn	(动)	be in hospital, be hospitalized	L15-S
转	zhuǎn	(动)	transfer	L8-S
桌子	zhuōzi	(名)	desk	L3
准备	zhǔnbèi	(动)	prepare	L5
咨询	zīxún	(动)	consult	L11
自己	zìjǐ	(代)	oneself	L14
自动取款机	zìdòng qǔkuǎnjī		Automatic Teller Machine (ATM)	L13-S
总机	zǒngjī	(名)	telephone exchange	L8-S
走	zǒu	(动)	walk	L3 S
足球	zúqiú	(名)	football	L14
最	zuì	(副)	most	L10
最近	zuìjìn	(名)	recentness	L6
昨天	zuótiān	(名)	yesterday	L6
左	zuǒ	(名)	left	L3-S

Chinese Crash Course

左右	zuǒyòu	（名）	about	L5
坐	zuò	（动）	take seat	L9
座	zuò	（量）	seat	L3-S
做	zuò	（动）	do	L14

专有名词
Proper Nouns

艾玛	Àimǎ	Emma	L1-S
澳大利亚	Àodàlìyà	Australia	L1
北京	Běijīng	Beijing	L6
成龙	Chéng Lóng	Jackie Chan	L14
大卫	Dàwèi	David	L1
俄罗斯	Éluósī	Russia	L1-S
法国	Fǎguó	France	L1-S
韩国	Hánguó	South Korea	L1-S
HSK 考试	HSK kǎoshì	HSK test	L11
（汉语水平考试）	(Hànyǔ Shuǐpíng Kǎoshì)		
刘涛	Liú Tāo	Liu Tao	L8
美国	Měiguó	America	L1
日本	Rìběn	Japan	L1-S
瑞典	Ruìdiǎn	Sweden	L1-S
四川	Sìchuān	Sichuan	L7
特快专递(EMS)	tè kuài zhuān dì (EMS)	EMS	L12
王宇	Wáng Yǔ	Wang Yu	L1

Proper Nouns

英国	Yīngguó	Great Britain	L1
中国	Zhōngguó	China	L1
中国工商银行	Zhōngguó Gōngshāng Yínháng	Industrial and Commercial Bank of China	L13
中国农业银行	Zhōngguó Nóngyè Yínháng	Agricultural Bank of China	L13-S
中国银行	Zhōngguó Yínháng	Bank of China	L13

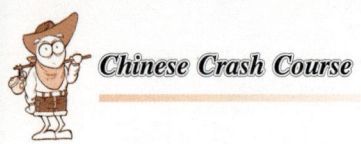

Chinese Crash Course

Appendix 1

语法术语对照表

Abbreviations of Chinese Grammatical Terms

名词	（名）	míngcí	noun (n.)
代词	（代）	dàicí	pronoun (pron.)
动词	（动）	dòngcí	verb (v.)
助动词	（助动）	zhùdòngcí	auxiliary verb (auxil. v.)
形容词	（形）	xíngróngcí	adjective (adj.)
数词	（数）	shùcí	numeral (num.)
量词	（量）	liàngcí	measure word (mw)
副词	（副）	fùcí	adverb (adv.)
介词	（介）	jiècí	preposition (prep.)
连词	（连）	liáncí	conjunction (conj.)
助词	（助）	zhùcí	particle (part.)
叹词	（叹）	tàncí	interjection (interj.)
拟声词	（拟声）	nǐshēngcí	onomatopoeia (onom.)
词头/前缀	（头）	cítóu/qiánzhuì	prefix (pref.)
词尾/后缀	（尾）	cíwěi/hòuzhuì	suffix (suf.)
专有名词	（专名）	zhuānyǒu míngcí	proper noun (pn)
主语	（主）	zhǔyǔ	subject (subj.)
谓语	（谓）	wèiyǔ	predicate (pred.)
宾语	（宾）	bīnyǔ	object (obj.)
定语	（定）	dìngyǔ	attribute (attrib.)
状语	（状）	zhuàngyǔ	adverbial (adv.)
补语	（补）	bǔyǔ	complement (compl.)

Appendix 2

常用反义词
Common Antonyms

大——小	多——少	远——近
dà xiǎo	duō shǎo	yuǎn jìn
big small	many few	far near

高——低	先——后	长——短
gāo dī	xiān hòu	cháng duǎn
high low	before after	long short

深——浅	真——假	冷——热
shēn qiǎn	zhēn jiǎ	lěng rè
deep shallow	true false	cold hot

粗——细	浓——淡	强——弱
cū xì	nóng dàn	qiáng ruò
thick thin	thick light	strong weak

软——硬	快——慢	薄——厚
ruǎn yìng	kuài màn	báo hòu
soft hard	quick slow	thin thick

胖——瘦	轻——重	干——湿
pàng shòu	qīng zhòng	gān shī
fat thin	light heavy	dry wet

Appendix 3

汉字书写
Chinese Writing System

一、笔画 Strokes

笔画是汉字结构的最小单位,基本笔画有八种。

Strokes are the smallest units of Chinese characters, and there are eight basic strokes.

(1) 横 héng Horizontal stroke

Example characters:

 (one)　　 (two)

(2) 竖 shù Vertical stroke

Example characters:

 (dry)　　 (ten)

(3) 撇 piě Left-falling stroke

Example characters:

 (eight)　　 (human)

Appendix 3

(4) 捺　　nà　　Right-falling stroke

Example characters:

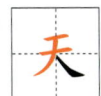 (sky)　　 (big)

(5) 点　　diǎn　　Dot

Example characters:

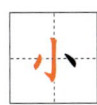 (small)　　 (main)

(6) 提　　tí　　Rising stroke

Example characters:

 (practice)　　 (beat)

(7) 折　　zhé　　Turning stroke

Example characters:

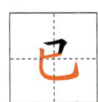 (already)　　 (bow)

(8) 钩　　gōu　　Hook

Example characters:

 (at; of; in)　　 (water)

Chinese Crash Course

二、笔顺　Strokes Order

写字的时候,笔画的先后次序叫做笔顺。一般规律为:
Stroke order is the order of strokes observed in Chinese calligraphy, the common rules are:

(1) 先横后竖　xiān héng hòu shù

Write the horizontal stroke before the vertical one

十　　　shí

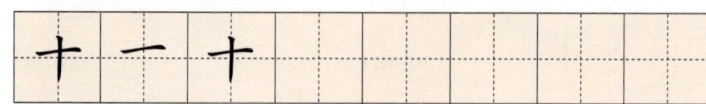

(2) 先撇后捺　xiān piě hòu nà

Write the left-falling stroke before the right-falling one

八　　　bā

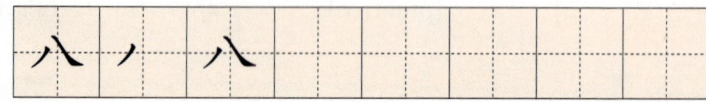

(3) 先上后下　xiān shàng hòu xià

Write from top to bottom

二　　　èr

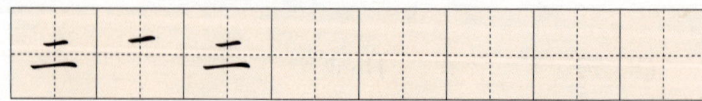

Appendix 3

(4) 先左后右　　xiān zuǒ hòu yòu

Write from left to right

仁　　rén

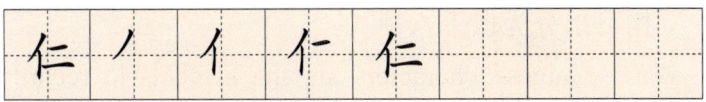

(5) 先外后内　　xiān wài hòu nèi

Write the outside before the inside

用　　yòng

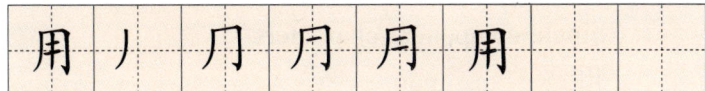

(6) 先中间后两边　　xiān zhōngjiān hòu liǎngbiān

Write the center before the two sides

水　　shuǐ

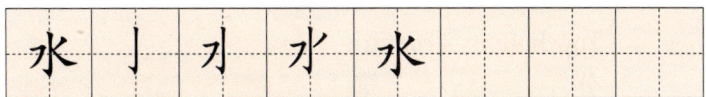

(7) 先里头后封口　　xiān lǐtou hòu fēngkǒu

Write the inside before enclosing

目　　mù

三、结构　Structures of Chinese Characters

汉字是记录汉语的文字。整体字形呈方块形,掌握好汉字的间架结构对汉字的书写非常重要。汉字的间架结构可以分为以下八种:

Chinese characters are the symbols to record Chinese language. A character is square-shaped. It's important to remember the 8 structures of Chinese characters before writing.

(1) 独体字　　　　　*dútǐzì*

　　Single-component characters
　　田　　*tián*

| 田 | 丨 | 冂 | 日 | 甶 | 田 | | |

(2) 上下结构　　　　*shàng-xià jiégòu*

　　Top-bottom structure
　　分　*fēn*　　草　*cǎo*　　念　*niàn*

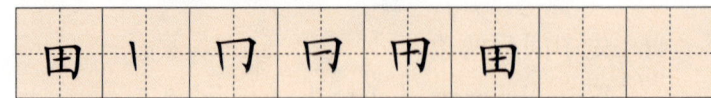

Appendix 3

(3) 上中下结构　　　　shàng-zhōng-xià jiégòu

Top-middle-bottom structure

京　jīng　　　　受　shòu

京	一	亠	京				
受	爫	爫	受				

(4) 左右结构　　　　zuǒ-yòu jiégòu

left-right structure

林　lín　　　　他　tā　　　　都　dōu

林	木	林					
他	亻	他					
都	者	都					

(5) 左中右结构　　　　zuǒ-zhōng-yòu jiégòu

left-middle-right structure

树　shù　　　　做　zuò

树	木	权	树				
做	亻	估	做				

Chinese Crash Course

(6) 半包围结构　　　bànbāowéi jiégòu
Semi-enclosed structure

| 同 | tóng | 画 | huà | 区 | qū |
| 厌 | yàn | 过 | guò | 匀 | yún |

同	丨	冂	同	同			
画	一	亩	画				
区	一	乂	区				
厌	厂	厌					
过	寸	过					
匀	丿	勹	匀				

(7) 全包围结构　　　quánbāowéi jiégòu
All-enclosed structure

园　yuán

| 园 | 囗 | 园 | 园 | | | | |

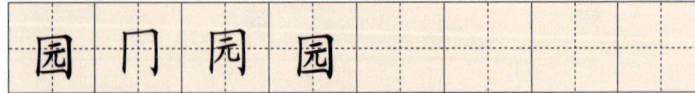

(8) 品字形结构　　pǐnzìxíng jiégòu

"品"-shape characters

淼　miǎo

淼	水	汆	淼				

汉字中,有些字比较特殊,很难按照上述规则书写,只能按笔顺来写,例如:"女"。还有些字比较复杂,不能只按一种规则书写,而要用几种规则来写,例如:"木"。学习时对这些字要着重记忆。

There are some special Chinese characters which are not written according to these rules, but they are written according to the stroke orders, for example, 女. There are also some complex characters. More than one rule needs to be followed when writing them, for example, 木. These characters should be paid special attention to.